# Seers and Scientists

# Seers and Scientists

## CAN THE FUTURE BE PREDICTED?

### *by* Ann E. Weiss

ILLUSTRATED WITH
DRAWINGS BY PAUL PLUMER
AND WITH PHOTOGRAPHS

**HBJ** *San Diego  New York  London*

HARCOURT BRACE JOVANOVICH, PUBLISHERS

Library of Congress Cataloging-in-Publication Data
Weiss, Ann E., 1943–
Seers and scientists.
Bibliography: p.
Includes index.
Summary: Discusses the phenomenon of predicting the
future, its history, philosophy, dangers, and
different methods both mystical and scientific, from
ancient arts such as astrology to modern
weather forecasting and the study of earthquakes.
1. Forecasting—Juvenile literature. [1. Forecasting]
I. Plumer, Paul, 1936–  ill.  II. Title.
CB158.W46  1986    303.4′9    86-11964
ISBN 0-15-272850-3

Designed by Barbara DuPree Knowles

Printed in the United States of America

First edition
A B C D E

# Contents

# O·N·E

# Prediction: Past and Present

**S**lowly, reverently, the *bûrû*—the seer—crosses the broad sunlit courtyard of the Ekur, the mighty temple at Nippur. Here is the dwelling place of Enlil, "the father," god of the air and of the atmosphere.

The Ekur's burned brick walls—red, brown, and black—contrast brilliantly with the rich blue of azure-enameled bricks and glowing lapis lazuli. Blue is Enlil's color. At one end of the courtyard, and rising high above it, is the ziggurat, a jagged tower of caked mud and brick. Inside, at the very top, is Enlil's shrine. Its golden table and comfortable couch await the god's pleasure. From the ziggurat, the entire city of Nippur is visible. So, too, is much of the fertile Euphrates River Valley in which the city lies.

Below, in the courtyard, the bûrû continues the ritual. Unlike most of the other men who have gathered to watch, the holy man is clean shaven. Like the others, however, he wears a skirt, long and flounced, made of a woven material. His feet are bare.

Prayerfully, the bûrû goes about his task. The sacrificial animal, a lamb, is made ready. The moment comes, the knife flashes, the animal groans. It is all for the glory of Enlil. Perhaps the words of the hymn run through the bûrû's mind:

"Without Enlil . . .
No cities would be built, no settlements founded,
No stalls would be built, no sheepfolds established,
No king would be raised, no high priest born,
No *mah*-priest, no high priestess, would be chosen by sheep-omen."

It is for the sake of the sheep-omen that today's ritual is being carried out. The *lugal*, or king, is planning to establish a new town farther downriver. Will the town prosper? Where is the best place to build, safe from storm and flood? How heavily must the city be fortified to protect its people from marauding foreigners? How many roads will be needed? How many irrigation ditches? All this the lugal must know before he can go ahead.

It is the sheep-omen that will provide the answers. Even now, the bûrû

*A hepatoscopist of long-ago Sumer prepares to predict the future.*

is examining the liver of the sacrificed animal. He has been long and carefully trained in the art of hepatoscopy—inspection of the liver. In that organ's blood, in its elaborate pattern of arteries, capillaries, and veins, he will seek the answers to his lugal's questions. Hepatoscopy will allow him to penetrate the veil that usually conceals the future from mortal men and women. Through his art, the bûrû will share in the foreknowledge of Enlil, "the lord whose pronouncement is unchangeable, who forever decrees destinies . . ."

Enlil is gone now, his name remembered only by a few scholars of the ancient world. He was but one of the thousands of gods worshipped long ago in the land of Sumer, in Mesopotamia. Today we call Mesopotamia, the land between the Tigris and Euphrates rivers, the "cradle of civilization." It was here, nearly 4,500 years ago, that Rimush and Manishtushu, sons of the Sumerian conqueror-king Sargon the Great, built Enlil's temple at Nippur. Yet even then, hepatoscopy was very old. For perhaps as much as a thousand years, Sumerian bûrûs had been turning to the sheep-omen to predict future events.

Halfway around the world and forty-five centuries later, men and women gather in a huge echoing room. Here is no artistically arranged brickwork, no glowing enamel, no precious stone. Instead, there is a hard concrete floor, an immensely high ceiling, the harsh glare of industrial lighting, and, in the center of the room, a slab of concrete. Measuring twenty feet on each side, the slab weighs twenty tons.

Atop the slab is a concrete-block wall, twenty-five feet high and ten feet wide. Dangling from top to bottom along its sides are massive steel cables. Wires, anchored to the wall by small silvery sensors, reach to the floor.

"Five, four, three, two, one." As the countdown ends, the slab begins to move. Hydraulic pistons, located underneath the concrete structure, cause it to shift back and forth and up and down. The wall shifts, too. It shakes to and fro, snapping the great cables, activating the sensors. For fifteen seconds the motion continues. Then it stops, and the waiting men and women start to examine the wall, searching for signs of damage.

No bûrû is among them, of course. These people are scientists with the Earthquake Engineering Research Center (EERC) at the University of California in Berkeley. The experiment they have been conducting took place in 1984. It was part of a joint United States–Japanese project aimed at determining what kinds of building materials and designs are best suited to withstand severe earthquakes.

A model of a seven-story reinforced concrete building sits atop the shaking table at the Earthquake Engineering Research Center at the University of California at Berkeley. Both will help scientists learn to predict which building materials and designs are best for withstanding quakes. (V. BERTERO, UNIVERSITY OF CALIFORNIA, BERKELEY)

The kind of thought and planning that went into the experiments at the University of California is very different from the assumptions that underlay the ancient art of hepatoscopy. The Sumerians had a mystic faith in the significance of the liver. To them it was the body's most essential organ, the seat of life. Equally mystical was their belief that in the livers of sheep could be read the future as it had been laid out by Enlil at the beginning of time.

There was nothing mystical about the 1984 experiments at Berkeley. The concrete slab, the pistons under it, the wall on top of it—all were constructed according to the most exacting scientific specifications. Sophisticated computers calculated every one of the pistons' moves, timing and directing them to reproduce as precisely as possible the stresses and strains a building would undergo during a real-life earthquake. The experiment described here, for example, created forces similar to those of the quake that destroyed much of San Francisco in 1906. Other sensitive machines recorded just how well various types of structures stood up to the simulated earth tremors. Through such rigorous testing, the scientists at the EERC hope to learn how to make buildings earthquake-proof. One day they may be able to tell city planners and construction engineers exactly what to do to guarantee the safety of people who live and work in earthquake zones.

And that's what links the modern scientists to the bûrûs of long-ago Sumer. Using the most up-to-date tools and techniques, they are trying to look ahead, to plan for secure towns and cities. The bûrûs, through hepatoscopy, were attempting to do the same thing. Predicting the future with hepatoscopy is vastly different from predicting it by means of scientific experimentation, but the purpose behind each method—to catch a glimpse of the future and to try to prepare for that future—is the same.

Today, as in the remotest days of human history, people are driven by a desire to look ahead in time. That desire is perpetual, whether we seek the future in science or mysticism; in experimentation or hepatoscopy; in a political poll or a gypsy's crystal ball; in a computer-generated weather forecast or a horoscope. "Human life," said José Ortega y Gasset, the twentieth-century Spanish philosopher, "is a constant preoccupation with the future." That preoccupation is as old as humanity itself.

# Ancient Arts

Long, long ago, back at the farthest reaches of human memory, there lived in the land of Sumer a wise and good king named Enmenduranna. For 28,000 years, or so the ancient myths tell us, Enmenduranna ruled his people judiciously. He was a great lawgiver who also possessed the godlike ability to see ahead in time. Enmenduranna used both talents to lay down the foundations of human civilization.

When he died, Enmenduranna passed on his gift for foretelling the future to those who followed him, and for centuries after, Sumerian bûrûs were honored as the Sons of Enmenduranna. It was they who painstakingly developed the rituals of hepatoscopy.

In a later time, the myth goes on, one of the Sons of Enmenduranna predicted a terrible flood. Prudently, he built a large boat. The inundation happened as foretold, and the prophet and his family rode it out while all others perished. Many modern scholars believe that this flood is the same one described in the Bible.

The floodwaters receded, and the towns of Sumer were rebuilt. Civilization became more sophisticated. Writing was invented, and with it began the recording of human history. Sumerian scribes worked at gathering the old stories, legends, and superstitions of their people and setting them down on clay tablets in the wedge-shaped script we call cuneiform.

Cuneiform tablets were also used to preserve the wisdom of the Sons of Enmenduranna. Archaeologists digging in what are today the countries of Iraq and Syria have uncovered hundreds of prophetic inscriptions. More than seven hundred are hepatoscopic. The archaeologists have also found clay models of livers. They believe that the bûrûs used the models to train their young pupils in the principles of hepatoscopy.

For thousands of years, hepatoscopy persisted. Even after 2000 or so B.C., when physicians decided that the heart, rather than the liver, was the seat of life, seers continued to practice hepatoscopy. The people of ancient Rome relied heavily upon it and upon the related art of reading the future in the arrangement of the intestines of animals. By about A.D. 500, though, doctors were beginning to understand that it is neither the liver nor the heart but the brain that is the source of thought and knowledge. With that, faith in hepatoscopy and the study of animal entrails waned. Only in a few remote areas of Uganda, Borneo, and Burma did those ancient arts survive into the twentieth century.

Although hepatoscopy was the most common method of prediction in Sumer, it was not the only one. The Sons of Enmenduranna also sought the future in the skies above them. Night after night, they entered the temples of the gods and climbed the towering ziggurats to gaze wonderingly at the brilliant heavens. Over the ages, the watchers observed the movements of the stars and planets, and with time they learned to predict their regular rising and setting.

This regularity must mean something, they thought. The orderly changes above must reflect orderly changes here on earth, changes like the passing of the months and the succession of the seasons. Perhaps the movements of the stars even caused those changes. Perhaps they were responsible for other changes and events, too—unsettling events like storms and floods and droughts. So reasoned the Sumerians of five thousand years ago, and so astrology was born.

From Sumer, astrology traveled to Egypt. Like the Sumerians, the ancient Egyptians used it primarily to foretell natural happenings in the sky and on earth and to predict climate and weather changes. It was probably the Egyptians who came up with the idea of the zodiac, the imaginary band of twelve constellations or "signs" that, astrologers say, govern human destiny.

Unlike hepatoscopy, astrology did not prove to be a dead end—it worked. Not only could its practitioners predict regular changes in the sky and in the seasons, but they were also learning to warn of unusual phenomena such as eclipses of the sun and moon. Knowing in advance that when either of the sky's brightest lights disappeared it would quickly and invariably reappear must have been a tremendous comfort to the ancients. Unexpected

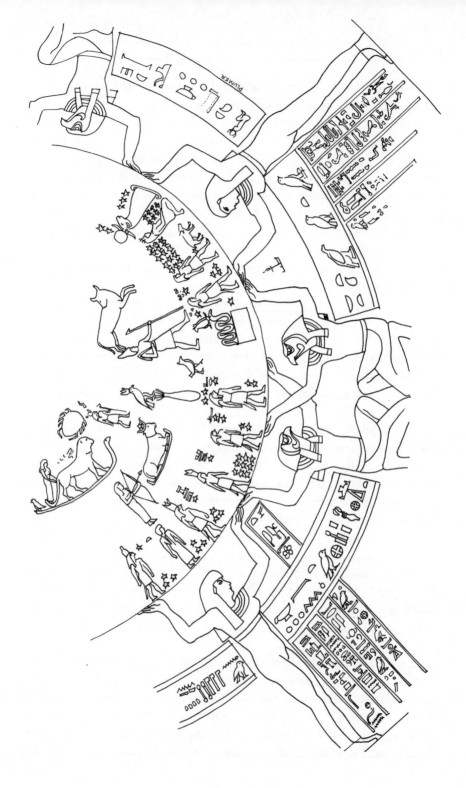

A zodiac from ancient Egypt (left) shows how astrologers of that time and place envisioned the stars and planets they believed allowed them to foretell the future. The archer (right) is a detail from another part of that zodiac. A zodiac from long-ago China (above) and (below) one engraved by the fifteenth-century German artist Albrecht Dürer.

eclipses have always been regarded by the unknowing as terrifying signals that the world was about to end.

Time went by, and astrology worked its way eastward from Egypt to India and eastward again to China. By the sixth century B.C., Chinese astrology was a highly developed art that even the philosopher Confucius cautioned people to respect. "Heaven sends down its good or evil omens," he wrote, "and wise men act accordingly." Yet Chinese astrology had its lapses. On one occasion, the emperor ordered his court astrologers Hi and Ho executed after they failed to predict a solar eclipse.

Astrology flourished in the western world, too. Between 600 and 200 B.C., Greek and Roman astrologers introduced the idea of horoscopes full of specific information about a person's future life and fortunes. These earliest horoscopes were elaborately and individually worked out according to intricate formulas based on the positions of the stars and planets at the moment of a person's birth.

Not until the ninth century A.D. did a simpler means of casting horoscopes come along. By then, astrology had established itself in Persia and other Arab lands. The major Arab contribution to astrology was the system of twelve "houses" worked out by the famed al-Battani. As al-Battani charted them, each house represented certain human characteristics. Once the astrologer knew into which house a person had been born, predicting his or her future was merely a matter of reading the charts aright.

Al-Battani's simplification helped turn astrology into a fad in Europe. By the twelfth century, kings and princes were hiring official astrologers to advise them when to make war, whom to marry, when to sue for peace. Doctors were checking with astrologers before ordering treatment, and the leading universities had astrologers on their faculties as a matter of course. Even some of the popes of medieval Europe confessed to consulting the stars.

For nearly five hundred years, astrology continued in vogue. Then came changes. People began hearing about new scientific findings, including surprising discoveries about the locations and relationships of the stars and planets. Thus began the science of astronomy, which was to become an important means of prediction in its own right.

By the mid-seventeenth century, astronomers had proved that many of the astrologers' old notions about the movements and significance of the heavenly bodies were wrong. For example, astrologers place the earth at the center of the solar system. Astronomers know that the sun is at its heart.

Facts like this shook people's belief in astrology, much as the medical discoveries of an earlier age had shaken their confidence in hepatoscopy.

Even so, astrology did not go the way of the sheep-omen. Its principles and symbols had so strong a grip on the human imagination that they managed to withstand the onslaughts of science. Throughout the eighteenth and nineteenth centuries, a few astrologers continued to practice their art, and by early in the twentieth century, this ancient tool of prediction was beginning to enjoy a revival.

One twentieth-century figure who claimed to rely upon the stars to guide his actions was Adolf Hitler, dictator of Germany from 1933 to 1945. Like the kings of old, Hitler appointed his own personal astrologers to offer him advice and warn him of danger. He credited one of them, Karl Ernst Krafft, with saving his life on November 11, 1939.

Krafft, so Hitler said, told the Nazi leader that an assassination attempt would be made against him as he delivered a speech in a beer hall in Munich on that date. Heeding the astrologer's advice, Hitler and his party left the hall earlier than planned—just twelve minutes before a bomb went off at the base of a pillar behind the rostrum from which he had spoken. Seven people died in the blast and thirty-three others were injured, but Hitler was safely on his way back to Berlin.

Another who attested to the value of astrology was the American Wallis Warfield Simpson. When Wallis was a young woman, an astrologer told her that she would have three husbands and that she would attain substantial power through a man. It happened like that, Wallis wrote in her memoirs. In 1936, after two marriages and two divorces, she became engaged to England's King Edward VIII. The two were married the next year.

Twentieth-century astrologers can point to other remarkable predictions. In 1948, astrologer Charles Jayne forecast the election victory of United States President Harry S Truman over his challenger, Thomas E. Dewey. Jayne's prediction seemed laughable when he made it; hardly a person in the country thought Truman had the slightest chance of winning. But win he did.

The astrology revival continues today. Hundreds of newspapers around the country carry a daily horoscope. Dozens of astrological books and articles appear each year, and astrological predictions show up frequently in the tabloid-type papers on sale at supermarket and convenience store checkout counters. Cable television stations carry astrological programs as well. A 1985 poll revealed that 55 percent of American teenagers believe that astrology, the ancient art of Sumer, can show what the future holds for them.

The Sumerians had one other method of seeking the future. This was dream interpretation. In fact, the very first prediction the Sumerians ever put into writing came in the form of a dream.

The prediction is found in an epic poem written six thousand years ago about the Sumerian hero Gilgamesh. In the poem, Gilgamesh dreamed of his approaching enemy Enkidu. Enkidu was a foreigner, a member of a fierce Semitic tribe. In Gilgamesh's dream, he and Enkidu fought to the death. Taking this as an omen, Gilgamesh grimly prepared himself for the final battle.

But Ninsun, Gilgamesh's mother, interpreted the dream differently. Her son and Enkidu would grow to be friends, Ninsun predicted, and she was right. Enkidu the Semite and Gilgamesh the Sumerian became inseparable. Their friendship foreshadowed what was to happen in Sumer when it was invaded by the Semites—ancestors of the ancient Hebrews—in about 4000 B.C. After a period of warfare, the two groups settled down to live in peace.

Like astrology, dream interpretation moved from Sumer to Egypt. The Egyptians regarded the dreams of their pharaohs as having special meaning, and their scribes recorded hundreds of them in their hieroglyphic picture writing. Two even found their way into the Bible. In the Book of Genesis, we read about Pharaoh's dream of seven lean cattle and seven fat ones, and of seven plump ears of corn and seven poor ones. It was the Jewish slave Joseph who correctly interpreted the dreams to mean that God would send seven years of good harvests followed by seven years of famine.

Prophetic dreams were important to the ancient Greeks, too. Thousands of them regularly paid a fee that allowed them to sleep in temples where the gods promised to send them uniquely significant dreams. The Greek philosopher Plato was convinced that dreams provide a glimpse of the future. In A.D. 150, the Greek soothsayer Artemidorus of Daldis wrote a book about dream symbols and meanings to help ordinary people interpret the images of sleep.

In more modern times, too, many have maintained that dreams bespeak events, particularly disastrous events, to come. On May 3, 1812, a mining engineer in Cornwall, England, reportedly told his wife of a dream in which he saw British Prime Minister Spencer Perceval shot to death in the House of Commons. Nine days later, Perceval was dead, assassinated in the Commons lobby.

One of the eeriest of all prophetic dreams was that recounted by President Abraham Lincoln in the presence of his wife Mary and several members of his White House staff in April 1865. As Lincoln remembered it, he dreamed that he was awakened by the sound of sobbing. In his dream, he saw himself get out of bed and go downstairs, where he found a coffin surrounded by mourners. "Who is dead?" he asked. "The president," came the response, "killed by an assassin." Days later, Lincoln was shot to death. Other disasters said to have been foretold in dreams include the murder of a nineteenth-century English girl, the 1922 killing of a British soldier by Irish terrorists, and a volcanic eruption that destroyed thousands of lives on the French island of Martinique in 1890.

Besides the prophetic dreams that haunt sleepers, there are those that come to the waking—the visions of the inspired and the scenes of the future witnessed by men and women in a state of trance. Visions may be linked to religious experiences, and many believe that the prophets of the Old and New Testaments were divinely inspired in their utterances. Millions of devout Christians and Jews believe that their prophecies—prophecies of the arrival of the Messiah, of the Second Coming of Christ, of the end of the world—have been, or yet will be, fulfilled.

Joan of Arc was a religious visionary. The saints and angels who appeared to her as a girl in the French village of Domrémy-la-Pucelle during the 1420s told her that she was fated to assume command of the French army, ensure that the Dauphin become king, and defeat the English invaders of her native land. Despite the disbelief she met, Joan persisted in following her visions. The French prince was crowned, and the English withdrew from much of France.

Not every vision has a religious origin. Many of those attributed to the legendary sixteenth-century English prophet known as Mother Shipton contained nothing of religion:

> "Around the world thoughts shall fly
> In the twinkling of an eye,
> Through hills men shall ride
> And no horse or ass at their side,
> Underwater men shall walk, . . .
> In the air shall men be seen,
> Carriages without horse shall go,
> And accidents fill the world with woe . . . "

This prophetic verse has awed thousands since it came to light in the nineteenth century. All that Mother Shipton seemed to predict—telegraph, railroad tunnels, underwater exploration, airplanes, and automobiles, even auto accidents—has come to pass.

Visionaries also exist in our own time. Jeane Dixon, an American born in 1918, claims to have had scores of accurate visions of the future. She says, for example, that in November 1944 she warned President Franklin D. Roosevelt that he would die within six months. At the time, an apparently healthy Roosevelt had just won his fourth term of office. He died the next April.

Seven years later, Jeane Dixon had a prophetic vision involving another president. In her own words, "Suddenly the White House appeared before me in dazzling brightness . . . the numerals 1–9–6–0 formed about the roof. . . . Then I looked down and saw a young man, tall and blue-eyed, crowned with a shock of thick brown hair . . .

"I was still staring at him when a voice came out of nowhere, telling me softly that this young man, a Democrat, to be seated as president in 1960, would be assassinated while in office . . . " The first part of that vision came true in 1960, when Democrat John F. Kennedy won the presidency of the United States. The second part was fulfilled—tragically—three years later with Kennedy's assassination in Dallas, Texas. Dixon also claims to have predicted the murders of Kennedy's brother Robert and of civil rights leader Martin Luther King, Jr.

According to Jeane Dixon, her visions come to her through a form of ESP, extrasensory perception. (However, she also bases some of her predictions upon readings in a crystal ball.) ESP is an aspect of parapsychology, which the dictionary defines as "the study of mental phenomena not explainable by accepted principles of science." Besides studying the kind of visions Jeane Dixon says she experiences, parapsychologists investigate such matters as poltergeists, apparitions, and telepathy. Important centers for the examination of parapsychology have been located at Duke University in North Carolina and the University of Utrecht in the Netherlands.

It is the parapsychologists at Utrecht who have looked into the claims of two of the world's best-known ESP visionaries, Gerard Croiset and his son, Gerard, Jr. Gerard, Sr., born in 1910 in Holland, appeared to possess an uncanny ability to find missing objects and people. The police of several countries have successfully enlisted his help in finding people who have disappeared and in reconstructing the scenes of crimes.

One of Gerard, Jr.'s, most publicized successes involved the crash of a Uruguayan passenger plane high in the Andes Mountains on October 10, 1972. The plane was far off its course when it crashed, and afterward no sign of it could be found. Desperate, the families of some of those who had been aboard appealed to young Croiset. Placing his hands on a map of the area in which the plane had vanished, Croiset reported "seeing" the following: Before takeoff one of the passengers had trouble with an official about his passport; the pilot was not flying the plane at the time of the accident; the craft "lay like a worm with a crushed nose but no wings"; it had crashed near a "Danger" sign and not far from a village with white houses; the wrecked plane was on a mountainside surrounded by three other mountains and a lake.

Weeks passed with no sign of the wreck or its victims. Then, four days before Christmas, two exhausted and emaciated young men stumbled out of the snowy Andes into a green valley where peasants brought their stock to graze. They were survivors of the crash, and they reported that fourteen others were still alive in the mountains above. When rescuers arrived at the crash site, they found it—location, terrain, the appearance of the plane itself—just as Croiset had said it would be. Even the fact that the copilot had been at the controls and that there had been a passport mix-up were confirmed.

Still another acclaimed twentieth-century visionary was Edgar Cayce. Cayce is called the Sleeping Prophet because his were not waking visions, but images of the future that came to him while he rested in a trancelike, semihypnotic state.

Born in Kentucky in 1877, Cayce claimed to have been only six when he experienced his first trance. As an adult, he produced over eight thousand predictions, among them numerous forecasts of earthquakes, hurricanes, and tidal waves throughout the Pacific Ocean area. In one 1936 vision, he saw himself in the year 2100 traveling across the United States in a strange futuristic aircraft. At one point, the craft landed in the midst of a large city that was being rebuilt after the devastation of a great war. Cayce heard himself ask what the city was. "New York," someone replied, and Cayce realized that the city had been destroyed in a war that had begun in 1999.

Cayce was but one in a long line of prophesiers whose visions have come to them in states of altered consciousness. Others include the medicine men of the North American Indian tribes, the voodoo magicians of the West Indies, the shamans of central Asia, the witch doctors of Africa, and the

Romany gypsies gazing into their crystal balls. But of all those who have prophesied from trances, none has surpassed in reputation the oracles of ancient Greece.

Most famous of the Greek oracles was Pythia, the Oracle at Delphi. For over a thousand years, from the eighth century B.C. until the fourth century A.D., a succession of carefully selected high priestesses filled the role of Pythia.

Pythia dwelt in the Temple of Apollo on Mount Parnassus, northwest of Athens. There, seated upon a three-legged golden stool in an underground cavern, she received questioners and supplicants from far and wide. No one today is sure how Pythia induced her trances. Perhaps she breathed fumes from sulphur gas seeping into her chamber through cracks leading to chasms far below. Or she may have chewed the leaves of some potent herb. But however it happened, Pythia's trance built into a frenzy, and her prophecies were delivered in indistinct sounds and riddlelike phrases, which had to be translated into simpler language by the priests of the temple.

Since the entranced prophetess was believed to speak for the gods, her cryptic utterances were considered sacred. Mighty kings traveled long distances to consult her wisdom. One of them, the fabulously wealthy Croesus of Lydia (part of modern Turkey), visited the oracle in about 546 B.C. What would happen, Croesus asked, if he went to war against Cyrus, King of Persia? Pythia's answer: "A great kingdom shall fall." Reassured, Croesus set off for war—with the results we'll see in Chapter 4.

Eleven hundred years after the last oracle sat at Delphi, another eminent waking dreamer raised his prophetic voice. This was the French Michel de Nostredame, better known by the Latin form of his name, Nostradamus.

The prophecies of Nostradamus were first published in 1555. They consisted of ten "centuries," most of which contained a hundred roughly rhymed verses each. ("Century" comes from the Latin word *cent*, one hundred.)

In the first two verses of *Century I*, Nostradamus describes how he goes about inducing his trances and calling up his visions. Late at night and alone, he slips into his secret study. In this mystic room stands a brass tripod bearing a bowl of water. The prophet seats himself and sprinkles some of the water over his robe and foot, a ritual that joins him with the mystic otherworld. Then he stares, stares, into the shimmering liquid. Slowly, the enchantment grows. His hypnosis deepens. Images form and clarify. The future is one with the present . . .

*Visions of the future in a bowl of water. Did Nostradamus really predict the death of King Henri II, the Great Fire of London, and many other events of the past—and of time to come?*

Here, reflected in the sacred bowl, is Henri II, King of France since 1547. Nostradamus sees the king "overcome . . . on the field of battle in single combat . . . [his opponent] will put out his eyes in a cage of gold . . . then [the king dies] a cruel death."

Shadows of other visions flicker before his eyes:

"London burnt by fire in three times twenty plus six . . . "

"Near the harbor and in two cities
Will be two scourges the like of which have never been seen."

"The year 1999, seventh month,
From the sky will come a great King of Terror:
To bring back to life the great King of the Mongols.
Before and after War reigns happily."

Many of the prophecies of Nostradamus seem to have been uncannily on target. It was in 1556 that the prophet warned King Henri II's wife, Catherine de' Medici, of her husband's approaching fate. Catherine took the warning seriously, but Henri ignored it. Three years later, he was rash enough to engage in single combat during a tournament, a medieval festival that included the staging of mock battles. In the midst of the fight, the lance wielded by Henri's opponent penetrated the king's gold-visored helmet, striking his eyes. Ten agonizing days later, Henri died.

In 1666 (three times twenty plus six), fire broke out in London. Still known as the Great Fire over three centuries later, the conflagration raged for five days until nothing remained to be consumed.

In 1945, the Japanese cities of Hiroshima and Nagasaki were leveled by a horrifying and totally new weapon of war, the atomic bomb. Both cities are on the water.

What about Nostradamus's prediction for our future? Will 1999 see the outbreak of World War III, a war involving the Russians or the Chinese, either of whom could be Nostradamus's "great Mongols"? Is it possible that a medieval mystic has something to tell us about our own future? Can a visionary like Jeane Dixon predict what lies ahead, or can an astrologer or anyone else whose tools and methods of prediction may be traced back to the dawn of human history?

Or is it to science that we must look for a trustworthy vision of our future?

# The Science of Prediction

**T**he mystic side of prediction was born in the walled cities and colorful temples of ancient Sumer. Its scientific aspect may have begun with a throw of the dice.

Gambling was a popular pastime in seventeenth-century Europe, and it was a seventeenth-century gambler and mathematician, a Frenchman named Blaise Pascal, who is credited with helping to develop a method for scientifically predicting the outcome of what people had always thought of as a mere game of chance.

It all started in 1653, when one of Pascal's friends and fellow gamblers asked him to solve a theoretical problem. Suppose several people are playing a game of dice, the friend said. The game is interrupted in the middle of a round. At this point, each player has a certain share of the stakes, depending upon the outcome of earlier throws of the dice. That share would have kept changing as the game continued.

But now the game can't be continued. How, asked Pascal's friend, can the stakes be fairly distributed among the players?

Pascal realized that he was being asked to make a prediction. How likely was it that each particular player would have won the game if it had continued? The greater the chance of each one's winning, the larger his share of the stakes should be. This chance, or *probability*, could be predicted mathematically, Pascal found. Because the problem he was working on had to do with gambling, Pascal called his probability theory *aleae geometriae*—Latin for "the geometry of the die."

Other Europeans were similarly intrigued by probability theory. One was the Italian scientist Galileo Galilei, who lived from 1564 to 1642. It was Galileo who formulated the four fundamental laws of probability.

Galileo's first law states that if a certain number of events all have an equal chance of happening, then the probability of any one of them coming to pass can be expressed as a fraction. That fraction is written as one over the total number of equally possible events. As an example, think of the toss of a die. A die has six sides, and if it has not been tampered with or weighted, each of them has an equal chance of coming up in any one toss. There is one chance in six that a one will come up, one chance in six that a two will come up, and so on. According to Galileo's first law of probability, the chance that any particular number will come up is expressed as 1/6.

Galileo's second law of probability says that the more often a trial—such as the throw of a die—is conducted, the more closely the actual outcome will conform to the predicted outcome. If you toss the die six times, it is unlikely that you will throw a one, a two, a three, a four, a five, and a six. That is true even though the chance of throwing each number is the same—1/6. Just try it and see. But if you throw the die sixty times, you will almost certainly get several ones, several twos, and several threes, fours, fives, and sixes. You probably won't get exactly ten of each number, though. However, if you toss the die six hundred times, the chance of turning up each side of the die equally often increases still more. Galileo's third and fourth laws of probability are more complex than the first two. They concern the likelihood of events that do not have an equal chance of occurring.

The work that Galileo and Pascal did on probability was highly theoretical, but before long, people were putting it to practical use. Among the first to do so were members of the wealthy banking families of Florence, Italy. Their interest in the subject took the form of offers to sell insurance policies to the owners of the trading ships that plied the waters of the Mediterranean Sea.

Insure a sailing ship? How could it be done? the skeptics demanded. How could anyone guarantee that an insured ship would make it safely back to port? If it did not return, the cost to the insurer—who would have to pay the owner back for the loss of the ship—would be enormous. No one could make a profit on insurance, the scoffers said. True, astrologers or others might predict a safe voyage or a shipwreck, but as every hardheaded merchant and moneylender knew, such forecasts tended to be unreliable. Insurance was no more than a gamble, they muttered.

In a way, they were right. But remember that gambling itself obeys the laws of probability. Those laws can't tell a dice player *which* number will come up on any one toss, but they can predict the *chance* that any one will appear.

It's similar with insurance. No one can say for sure that this or that ship will complete its voyage. But how likely is it that every insured ship will sink? Not very. All the Florentine bankers had to do was to check past records to see how many ships sailed and how many sank, year after year. They could then calculate the probability of losing any one vessel over a period of time. Perhaps they would find that, on average, three ships sank for every hundred that sailed from a given port in a given year. That meant there were three chances in a hundred of losing a ship. The insurers would have no idea *which* ships were destined to sink, but that would not matter to them. What mattered was that while any ship's chance of sinking would be 3/100, the probability that it would return to port would be 97/100. Profits from selling insurance to the owners of the ninety-seven ships that successfully completed their voyages would more than cover the costs of replacing the three lost vessels.

From such beginnings, the insurance industry has grown into a worldwide multibillion-dollar business. Today we can insure ourselves against almost anything: death, illness, fire, theft, accidents, and so on. Ballet dancers have been known to insure themselves against strained muscles, and opera stars against strained vocal cords. Since its founding in 1688, insurers at the famed Lloyd's of London have sold people insurance against damage to a movie star's beard, the possibility of having twins, and hazards that might result from the capture of the Loch Ness Monster.

Every insurance policy is worked out according to a series of predictions. Before selling auto insurance to a customer, for instance, an insurance agent will try to predict whether or not that customer will be involved in a smashup. Is the customer a teenager? Statistics show that people in their teens have more accidents than adults. The accident record of teenage boys is especially bad. That's why teenage boys must often pay higher auto accident insurance rates than girls. In the same way, life insurance for a sixty-year-old will probably cost more than for a twenty-year-old; a person with a history of illness may find it difficult to buy health insurance; and anyone who owns a house on the Florida coast will pay dearly to be protected against damage from hurricanes. An insurer who cannot make accurate predictions about climate and weather, health and longevity, and the probability of accidents and unexpected events will soon be out of business.

To make such predictions, the insurer must have accurate information. Back in the days of the first Italian marine insurers, much of that information was lacking. Take weather information. Up to the middle of the seventeenth century, ship captains and the bankers who insured them had no way of predicting when storms and gales might beset their vessels at sea. What weather predictions there were came from astrologers or were based on folk sayings: Red sky at night, sailor's delight; a ring around the moon portends a storm. Such predictions might have a certain amount of truth and be useful in a general way, but they were not enough to prevent hundreds of wrecks, thousands of deaths, and a great loss of money.

Then, in 1643, came the first invention of modern meteorology—the barometer. It was designed by the Italian Evangelista Torricelli, and it allowed scientists to measure the pressure of the atmosphere. It wasn't long before the scientists spotted the relationship between atmospheric pressure and weather. High pressure meant fair weather; low pressure meant a storm was on the way.

To the barometer, weather scientists soon added the thermometer. Although the first crude instrument for measuring the temperatures of liquids had been invented by Galileo decades earlier, it was only when G. D. Fahrenheit introduced the mercury thermometer in 1714 that scientists had a tool for measuring air temperature. The Celsius thermometer came along about thirty years later.

The thermometer and the barometer were a boon to sailors and to others, such as farmers, whose livelihoods depended upon the weather. Now they could look beyond weather lore and astrology to science. Checking the barometer would tell them when air pressure was falling and a storm was coming. The thermometer would tell whether to expect rain or snow.

As the years went by, the science of weather forecasting became more and more precise. The telegraph, invented in the nineteenth century, permitted the rapid collection of weather data from many areas, and scientists began to see how weather changes in one part of the world affect weather in other parts. That discovery led them to investigate upper air currents and the circulation of the atmosphere. By the mid-twentieth century, they had a good understanding of both and of their relationship to climate and weather changes.

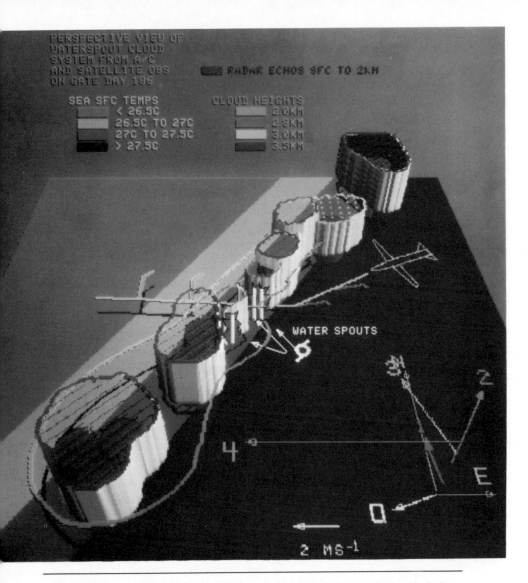

*A series of water spouts and the cloud system that produced them are made to look three-dimensional in this photograph. The images, constructed by a computer with data from aircraft and a weather satellite, can help forecasters make quick, accurate weather predictions.* (NASA / GODDARD SPACE FLIGHT CENTER)

Today that understanding is better than ever. Weather satellites circle the globe, taking pictures and sending them back to earth. Special infrared sensing devices gather information about moisture and temperature conditions throughout the atmosphere. Fed into computers back on earth, such information can be synthesized into three-dimensional images of clouds and storm systems.

The result is weather forecasts that grow more accurate with every year. Modern meteorologists can spot a hurricane while it is nothing more than a small low-pressure area in the tropical waters off the coast of Africa. In these low latitudes near the equator, weather systems move from east to west, and scientists can track the storm day by day as it moves westward across the Atlantic. Thus they are able to notify people days ahead of an expected landfall. Satellite photos and pictures taken from aboard aircraft are also useful in spotting and following blizzards. These large winter storms are similar in structure to hurricanes, though they do not always have an "eye" at the center.

More difficult to predict are the movements of tornadoes, violent storms that usually break out suddenly and may move erratically over wide areas. For these reasons, forecasters have found it hard to locate tornadoes even with radar. In the last half of the 1980s, however, meteorologists plan to test new, highly sophisticated radar systems believed to be capable of detecting most twisters. They hope to have 180 tracking stations equipped with the new technology in place by 1987.

The improvement in weather-forecasting techniques over the years means more than the convenience of knowing whether or not to carry a sweater or wear boots. It can be measured in lives saved and property damage averted. Compare, for example, two storms that hit the same stretch of the Texas Gulf Coast sixty-one years apart. The first, which struck on September 8, 1900, was totally unexpected. No forecast warned of its coming, and the storm killed 12,000 people. It was the worst natural disaster ever in United States history.

The second storm, Hurricane Carla, arrived in September 1961. Days before it reached the coast, Carla was spotted by cameras aboard an experimental weather satellite. Scientists at the National Weather Service warned 350,000 coastal residents to prepare to evacuate their homes and move inland to safety. As a result, only forty-six people lost their lives. Although Carla was a more powerful storm than the 1900 hurricane, it is not even mentioned in the *World Almanac* list of storm disasters.

Modern meteorologists can also look to outer space to help them predict the weather. Sunspots are one thing they look for.

Sunspots are magnetic disturbances—"storms"—deep inside the star itself. Since the temperature at the top of such a storm is lower than the temperature elsewhere on the sun, sunspots appear as dark patches on the solar surface. Scientists discovered sunspots soon after Galileo invented the telescope in 1609, but it was many years before they recognized their connection with our weather. Today scientists are well aware of the link, and they can predict that an increase in sunspot activity, which occurs approximately every twenty-two years, will be accompanied by an increase in the number of magnetic storms, such as thunderstorms, here on earth.

Galileo's invention of the telescope led to a new interest in studying the heavens, an interest with vast implications for the art of prediction. Astrology was about to be confronted by the new science of astronomy.

The earliest hints of the conflict between astrology and astronomy came even before Galileo's time, back in the days of the Polish astronomer Nicholas Copernicus. Copernicus, who lived from 1473 to 1543, was the first European to suggest that the earth circles the sun, rather than the other way around.

This observation badly upset the astrologers' fixed ideas. If the earth was not at the center of the universe, all their star charts must be in error. What's more, by the 1500s people were beginning to realize that, over the centuries, the sun's position was steadily shifting in relationship to the constellations of the zodiac. That discovery meant additional mistakes in the ancient charts. Yet astrologers were still using those charts to cast horoscopes. This practice naturally raised doubts in some people's minds about the value of astrology in predicting the future.

Some astrologers were among the doubters. Tycho Brahe, born in Denmark in 1546, and his thirty-year-younger associate, the German Johannes Kepler, both served as royal astrologers to the kings and nobles who employed them. But both were astronomers as well, and both made star observations that confirmed the inaccuracy of the astrological tables. Although Brahe never fully accepted the Copernican theory, Kepler did, and both eventually rejected astrology. Before he died in 1630, Kepler described the art as the "mad daughter" of astronomy, useful only to help support her poor but honorable mother.

From then on, the split between astronomy and astrology widened and deepened. By now, astrologers were fighting a rear-guard action, frantically trying to defend their outmoded charts and to explain away certain embarrassing predictions. One outstanding blunder was the detailed horoscope the sixteenth-century Italian astrologer Geronimo Cardano drew up for England's King Edward VI. Edward, Cardano said, would live to the age of fifty-five years, three months, and seventeen days, whereupon he would fall desperately ill. In fact, Edward, the frail young son of Henry VIII, died in 1553, aged sixteen. Cardano himself died twenty-three years later, under the strange circumstances we will look at in Chapter 4.

In the meantime, the predictions of the astronomers—whose precise science required them to steer clear of horoscopes and prognostications about human events—were proving to be startlingly accurate. In 1682, the English astronomer Edmund Halley calculated the path of the great comet that blazed across the sky that year. This was the same comet that had appeared over and over in the past, Halley claimed, and he predicted that it would return over and over in the future. Halley went so far as to announce the year in which it would next be seen, 1758 or 1759. In fact, he was right both ways. The comet appeared on Christmas night, 1758, and was visible well into the next year. Halley's comet, which flashed past the earth and whipped around the sun once more in 1985 and 1986, will not appear again until the year 2062.

Another predictive triumph for astronomy came in 1846, with the discovery of the planet Neptune. Two astronomers, J. C. Adams of England and U. J. Leverrier of France, working independently of each other, had noticed that the orbit of the planet Uranus wobbled inexplicably. Could there be another, unknown, planet beyond Uranus? Was this planet's gravity tugging at Uranus and causing those irregularities? Leverrier and Adams believed there was such a planet, and they even predicted exactly where it would be found. One astronomer who read Leverrier's prediction was Johann Gottfried Galle of the Berlin Observatory. The next night, Galle pointed his telescope at the spot Leverrier had specified—and saw Neptune. Eighty-four years later, the ninth solar planet, Pluto, was discovered in a similar manner.

Does still another planet lie somewhere out in the void beyond Pluto? Pluto itself appears to be too small to be causing the irregularities that scientists have observed in Neptune's orbit, and some of them predict that astronomers will discover yet a tenth planet.

The new attitude toward prediction that grew out of the scientific revolution of the seventeenth and eighteenth centuries had applications in other fields besides astronomy, meteorology, and insurance. Scientific prediction assumed a role in medicine, for instance, where consultations with astrologers were replaced by careful analyses of diseases and of their symptoms and possible cures. It helped spur the industrial revolution of the eighteenth and nineteenth centuries, as farsighted inventors began imagining and building machines for spinning thread and weaving cloth, for producing steam power and processing agricultural products, for refining ores and speeding up transportation. And in the world we know today, science and technology have made accurate prediction an everyday event. Year by year, throughout the twentieth century, our scientific prophets have tackled one new field after another.

One of those involves the kind of earthquake research we saw in Chapter 1. Another is earthquake prediction itself. Scientific earthquake prediction dates back less than twenty-five years and owes its origins to the theory of "plate tectonics," which scientists began developing in the 1960s. This theory states that the earth's crust consists of seven large, slow-moving segments or plates. The continent of Australia lies on one such plate. Most of the Pacific Ocean is on another.

In some parts of the world—California is one—two plates touch. Scientists refer to the boundary between the two as a fault. California's largest geological fault is the San Andreas Fault, which stretches down the coast from San Francisco to Los Angeles.

As two plates grind slowly past each other, at a rate of only an inch or two a year, rocks on either side of the fault come under an increasing strain. Eventually the strain builds to the breaking point. In a matter of seconds, great sections of the earth's crust heave and twist and fall apart. That's an earthquake.

In recent years, scientists have found ways to measure the strain along fault lines. By studying and analyzing their finds and comparing them to past earthquake records, they are learning how much strain is necessary to produce a quake. In April 1985, geologists with the United States Geological Survey (USGS) came up with their most precise earthquake prediction ever. According to the scientists, a quake should hit the town of Parkfield, California, sometime during 1988. Parkfield is located on the San Andreas Fault about halfway between Los Angeles and San Francisco, and the strain along that part of the fault underlying Parkfield will have become great enough to cause a moderately severe tremor by 1988.

Although earthquake prediction is a new science, it can already count at least one life-saving success. Late in 1974, Chinese geologists forecast a quake for the city of Haicheng in northeastern China. The city was evacuated, and two months later, in February 1975, the scientists' prediction came true. Haicheng was badly damaged, but there were few deaths or injuries.

Closely related to the science of earthquake prediction is the science of volcano prediction. Volcanic eruptions are often preceded by or followed by earthquake shocks. When, in 1980, quakes and tremors began shaking up an area of Washington state, geologists began anticipating the eruption of a dormant volcano there. Although the geologists did not feel confident enough to issue a specific volcano warning, they did advise residents and visitors to be wary. By midspring, it was clear that an eruption of the volcano—Mt. St. Helens—was imminent. Scientists asked everyone to leave the vicinity. Nevertheless, when the eruption occurred in late May, it killed about sixty people. Five years later, similar earthquakes and rumblings from deep underground alerted scientists to the possibility of volcanic activity in the South American nation of Colombia. Although the people there knew an eruption was possible, no precise warnings were given. In November 1985, the Colombian volcano killed 23,000 men, women, and children.

Another kind of scientific prediction, political polling, dates back to surveys conducted in the 1930s by an American named George Gallup. Most dramatic of modern political polls are those that tell us, weeks or months before an election, who the winner will be. Now much of the excitement of an election lies in waiting to see how accurately the pollsters have predicted its outcome.

Polling, like gambling or insurance, involves probability theory. The idea behind it is to select a small group or sample of people and question them about their ideas and attitudes on a particular subject. If the people in the sample have been chosen correctly, the answers they give will have a high probability of accurately reflecting the ideas and attitudes of a much larger group.

How is the group chosen correctly? In the first place, the selection is made at random, meaning that every person in the large group must have the exact same mathematical chance of being in the smaller group as every other person. No one must be discriminated against. However, avoiding any discrimination at all is more difficult than it sounds.

Imagine that researchers intend to conduct a poll in your town or city. They plan to interview, say, 900 people out of a total population of 54,000. At first it might appear that a logical approach would be to open the local telephone directory and get in touch with the first 900 people listed. Or, they might locate official voter-registration lists and talk to 900 men and women whose names are found there.

Neither method, however, will work. Neither will produce a random sample of the general population. The first will produce only a sample of those people in town who have both a telephone and a listed telephone number. It will discriminate against those who do not want a phone or cannot afford one, or those who have some reason (a busy lifestyle? local notoriety?) for avoiding a phone book listing. The second method, consulting voting lists, will yield a sample of the voting public, ignoring nonvoters or late registrants. Both methods will discriminate against people whose last names begin with a letter at the middle or end of the alphabet.

There is just one way to come up with a sample that is truly random, and that is to start with the names of every adult man and woman in the community. (With the name of every child, too, if children are to be included in the sample.) In a community of 54,000 adults, the list will be 54,000 names long. It will be in strictly alphabetical order.

To choose their random sample, the pollsters first divide the total population of 54,000 by the size of their projected sample, 900. That gives them a figure of sixty, so they will interview every sixtieth person on the alphabetized list. Instead of simply talking with the first person, then with the sixty-first, then with the one-hundred-twenty-first, however, the researchers add an extra precaution against discrimination by picking at random a number between one and sixty. Perhaps it is the number sixteen. That means that the sixteenth person on the list of 54,000 names becomes number one in the sample. Number two in the sample is number seventy-six on the original list, number three is one hundred thirty-sixth on the list, and so forth.

Selecting a sample at random guarantees a high probability that the sample will mirror the larger group faithfully. If the larger group is 52 percent female, the sample will be about 52 percent female, too. If 46 percent of the larger group failed to vote in the last election, 46 percent of the smaller group will probably have done the same.

Modern pollsters rely upon computers to do the huge job of drawing up the necessary alphabetized population lists. Computers also perform the mathematics needed to select the random sample. When every selection procedure is scrupulously followed, a sample need not be large. Professional pollsters routinely question as few as 1,200 or 1,500 men and women to learn the opinions of all 235 million Americans.

Strange as it may seem, this system works. It's rare for pollsters to be mistaken in their predictions of election winners. Polls can also tell us how we as a nation feel about social and economic problems: crime, pollution, the threat of nuclear war, unemployment, the national debt, and much more.

The results of such polls make interesting newspaper reading, but their usefulness transcends that. Candidates for political office may turn to the polls to learn what Americans think about the issues facing the country. This information can help them decide what positions to take on those issues. In addition, elected officials may study the polls to find out what new laws the country wants and needs.

The techniques of political polling are used in making other kinds of predictions. One United States business, the A. C. Nielsen Company, utilizes them to help predict which television and radio shows will be most popular in the coming weeks and months.

The television viewing information is especially valuable. By monitoring television sets in a few thousand randomly selected homes across the country, Nielsen researchers learn which programs are being watched by the greatest number of people. Network executives are glad to buy this information; the more popular a program is, the more they can charge advertisers to air their commercials during it. Advertising time during an unpopular program—one with a low Nielsen rating—may cost only a few thousand dollars per minute. A minute of advertising time during the 1986 Super Bowl football game, by contrast, cost $1.1 million. Even the kind of advertising that appears on a particular program may be determined by Nielsen findings. Before Super Bowl 1986 was broadcast, researchers predicted that many watchers would be truck drivers and owners. Result: a company that manufactures rubber mats for pickup truck beds—a company that had never before advertised on television—bought Super Bowl time.

Television network executives find Nielsen information useful in other ways. It alerts them to shifts in viewer interest from one type of show to another, and observing these shifts allows the executives to predict coming trends. If more and more people are watching comedies and fewer and fewer are tuning in to police shows, for example, network planners conclude that comedies will be more popular next year. Hastily, they call in their gag writers and comic stars.

Polling techniques also turn up in the marketplace. Before any new product is offered for sale, it goes through a process called test marketing.

The first step in the testing is to find out how consumers will feel about the proposed product. Would you chew gum that has a center of tooth-protecting fluoride? researchers ask. Wash silverware with a detergent that polishes as it cleans? Buy an "eraser" that removes makeup without mess? Use lemon-scented paper towels?

Once the manufacturers have—or think they have—an item people will buy, the product is made available in one or two cities or parts of the country. By watching how well it sells there, market analysts predict how well it will do elsewhere. Only after the analysts can say with confidence that the product will make a profit does its manufacturer place it on shelves in stores around the country.

Market research is a big business, a half-billion-dollar-a-year business in the United States, but it is only one kind of economic forecasting. Pick up any newspaper or magazine and you can read about dozens of others. One article mentions that the nation's factory owners have been placing large orders for new tools and equipment. Such orders mean they expect business to be good, economists say, and they go on to predict that many new factory jobs will soon be open to American workers. Other stories confirm the optimistic forecast. Prices on the stock market are going up. That rise, too, suggests that business will boom.

Most comprehensive of all modern United States economic forecasts is the federal budget. Worked out each year by the president and Congress, the budget is prediction on a grand scale.

Few of us think of it that way. But what else are lawmakers doing, as they debate and argue about how much to spend on weapons and military equipment, on education, on health care for the poor and elderly, on disaster relief and highway safety, and on all the other areas for which the federal government takes a financial responsibility? Nothing else but making predictions, predictions about America's future military demands, about its people's educational needs and about their health, about the likelihood of disastrous storms, floods, and fires, about the conditions of roads and bridges in every state, and much more. Each year's federal budget is a prediction that affects every one of us deeply.

In addition, predictions affect us in other ways that we rarely think about. Anyone who fastens an automobile seat belt does so because car manufacturers and safety experts have predicted that drivers and their passengers will be safer that way. If all of us used our belts, the experts say, close to 25,000 American lives would be saved each year. A person who takes an IQ (intelligence quotient) test or an aptitude test is helping teachers and psychologists to make predictions about his or her future achievements and accomplishments. People who move into a new house or apartment building accept the predictions of architect and builder that the structure will prove sound. The placement of city traffic lights is the end product of a complex of predictions about traffic flow, intersection hazards, and expected urban growth.

Sporting events are matters for prediction, too. On the eve of baseball's yearly World Series games, prediction runs rampant—and it's not just a matter of loyally betting on the home team, either. A good deal of scientific calculation can go into forecasting the outcome.

Which team has the better won-lost record over the season? That team may have an edge in the Series. On the other hand, that team may be exhausted, "played out." Which team has the better pitching staff, the better batting averages, the better fielding percentage? How do the players perform against right-handed pitchers as opposed to left-handed ones? Which will they face most often in the Series? If the Series goes a full seven games, one team will play on its home field four times, the other only three. Will that have an effect?

For days before the World Series begins, amateur and professional bettors weigh the statistics, ponder the variables, and consider the odds. Nor do they limit themselves to trying to predict winner and loser. One fan may bet that a team will win the World Series in five games; another will wager that it will take seven. At Super Bowl time, one may bet that a team will win by at least ten points; another that the point spread will be twenty.

From sports contests to the stars, from money to meteorology, from geology to government, prediction has come a long way in the last three hundred years. With the dawn of modern science in the seventeenth and eighteenth centuries, the art of prophecy began giving way to the science of prediction. Probability theory, the tools and instruments that permit exact measurement, and—most important of all—the scientific discipline that demands accuracy in observation and analysis, these factors are what allow our modern forecasters to show us a scientific vision of the future.

But is that vision enough? Or does the inspired prophecy of ages past still have something of value to offer us?

# How Accurate an Art?

"**W**ill I defeat King Cyrus of Persia in battle?" Croesus of Lydia asked the Oracle at Delphi.

Pythia's answer—that a great kingdom would fall if Croesus marched against his enemy—was all that that monarch needed to hear. His spirits high, he went confidently off to war.

His confidence was not misplaced. The oracle had spoken truly. A great kingdom did fall as the result of King Croesus's campaign against Cyrus. That kingdom was Croesus's own, however, and not his opponent's. In despair, the disillusioned and captive Lydian threw himself upon a blazing funeral pyre.

Pythia's prophecy to Croesus was typical of the Oracle at Delphi. The priestesses who presided at that shrine were known for responding to questions ambiguously, with words that could be interpreted in more ways than one. Croesus simply made the mistake of taking Pythia's prophecy to mean what he wanted it to mean, overlooking the fact that when two kings wage war, two kingdoms are at risk. Four hundred years later, the Roman philosopher, politician, and orator Marcus Tullius Cicero regarded the oracle with a more critical eye. One of her pronouncements, Cicero noted, could be taken to mean either, "You can conquer the Romans," or, "The Romans can conquer you." With a prediction like that, what prophet could fail?

Wrapping her prophecies in a cloak of ambiguity was one way the Oracle at Delphi built her reputation and maintained it for a thousand years. But the oracle did not rely upon equivocation alone. She had a host of wise and well-informed temple priests whose job it was to make her garbled phrases comprehensible to those who came to her seeking answers about the future.

Starting in the seventh century B.C., Delphi was the home of the Greek *amphictymy*, a religious league that served to unify the land's separate city-states. For eight centuries, until the Roman conquest of Greece, Delphi remained a vital center of Greek religious, political, social, and cultural activity.

The priests at Delphi observed that activity diligently. They kept tabs on friendships and enmities, on alliances and broken treaties, and on relations among the cities, their peoples, and their leaders. At the same time, they noted which people consulted Pythia and what they asked her about. Did this king speak of the possibility of war? Then perhaps he himself was preparing to do battle. Did that king ask about the chances of peace? Perhaps his city was weak, his subjects reluctant to fight. Patiently, the temple priests gathered each hint, every suspicion, all the information that came their way and shrewdly put it together to form a detailed picture of what was going on around Greece and in other parts of the Mediterranean world. Result: predictions of startling accuracy.

Many successful visionaries have relied, consciously or unconsciously, upon their awareness of current affairs. Take the hepatoscopists of ancient Sumer. To us today, it may seem ridiculous that anyone would believe that a sheep's liver holds the secrets of the future. And yet . . .

And yet the bûrûs prophesied well. Reading the sheep-omen, they chose good leaders for their people, designed cities and temples, planned military campaigns, and predicted floods and famine. How did they do it? Like the priests who would one day speak for the Oracle at Delphi, the bûrûs knew their world. They knew their country's military strength, its wealth, its people, its trade needs. They were familiar with its climate and its weather. Like the Delphic priests who would follow them, the bûrûs were skilled at turning their understanding of the present into a powerful vision for the future.

Of course, that vision depended upon the sheep-omen, for the bûrûs were genuine mystics who had every faith in their art. But the omen was chiefly a guide. If an animal's liver showed good fortune ahead, the bûrûs would have a clear idea where that good lay, whether in war or in peace, for example. If the organ indicated ill luck, the bûrûs' awareness of what was going on in the towns and cities of Sumer would tell them exactly against what danger the lugal should be warned.

Many of the predictions that came out of medieval Europe also displayed a knowledge of political affairs. Certainly the court astrologers of the Middle Ages were as familiar with the politics of their day as any bûrû or Delphic priest was with those of his. Nor did Nostradamus leave his political awareness behind as he made his nightly pilgrimage to the secret chamber. Many of Nostradamus's visions were political. Often, they concerned religious politics.

Religion was a serious issue in Nostradamus's Europe. The Protestant Reformation had begun early in the sixteenth century, and conflict between the new faith and the Roman Catholic Church was intense. Over and over, Nostradamus, a devout Catholic, predicted death and destruction for those who had turned to Protestantism. An example is his prophecy about the Great Fire of London. England had broken away from the Catholic Church in 1534, and that, to Nostradamus, seemed enough to merit punishment from heaven.

Modern visionaries may also turn to current events to help them make their predictions. In the fall of 1985, Jeane Dixon issued a series of forecasts, several of which had to do with politics. President Ronald Reagan would face a showdown with Congress over federal spending, Dixon said, and his problems in dealing with the Soviet Union would not be easily solved. A third prediction was that Soviet President Mikhail Gorbachev would make dramatic, but meaningless, proposals for nuclear disarmament.

If nothing else, Dixon's predictions showed that she was keeping up with the news. As most Americans were aware, President Reagan, a Republican, had been at odds with Democrats in Congress over budget matters since the day he took office in 1981. Most also knew that American and Soviet leaders have always had trouble getting along with each other and that Soviet leaders (and sometimes American leaders, too) have been making dramatic but meaningless nuclear disarmament proposals ever since the first atomic bombs were detonated in 1945.

But they showed more than that. They were an excellent demonstration of the way mystics may allow their own personal interests, beliefs, values, and prejudices to color the predictions they make.

Jeane Dixon is a patriotic American and a fervent anticommunist, and her prophecies reflect that bias. In 1948, for example, she predicted that American cities would experience race riots starting in the 1960s. She was right. But Dixon had said that the racial disturbances would be inspired by Communist agents working on behalf of the Soviet Union. There has been absolutely no evidence of that. Dixon also says that she predicted that civil rights leader Martin Luther King, Jr., would be assassinated by Communists. Again, she was right about the assassination, which took place in 1968. But she was mistaken about there being any Communist involvement. Dixon's anticommunism, and the way it keeps popping up in her predictions, resembles Nostradamus's antiprotestantism. Without doubt, the bûrûs of Sumer and the priests at Delphi permitted their political and religious attitudes to slip into their predictions from time to time, as well.

An awareness of current events and an understanding of political and religious trends are only part of the story, however. Knowledge or experience of any kind is helpful to those who try to peer ahead in time. The sailor who looks at a brilliant sunset and predicts fair weather is relying upon practical experience. Fair weather usually does follow a bright sunset. There is a good meteorological reason for this phenomenon. When we see a red sunset, we are seeing the sun's rays bouncing off tiny dust particles in the air. Those particles mean the air is dry; if it were wet and rainy, the particles would have been washed out. And since weather systems in the higher latitudes move from west to east, the fact that the air is dry where the sun is setting usually means that no storm is approaching. Of course, the sailor does not have to know all that in order to be right in his forecast. Experience is enough for him.

Common sense is another key to successful predictions. Consider the interpretation of dreams. If a king dreams that he loses a battle, it may be because he knows, in his heart of hearts, that his army is unprepared for war. If he dreams of the death of his young son, maybe it is because he has unconsciously observed the first signs of illness or weakness in the child. A prophet who uses his common sense will have little trouble interpreting such dreams.

Common sense comes to the astrologer's aid as well. The seer who drew up Wallis Warfield's horoscope and predicted that she would marry three times and win power through a man was employing it. The divorce rate was rising in the 1920s, and Wallis herself was divorcing her first husband at the time the prediction was made. According to the testimony of several who knew her, she was also already in love with Ernest Simpson, who was to be her second husband. That she would marry Simpson, and later divorce him to marry again, was by no means an unreasonable assumption. Neither was it unreasonable for an astrologer to guess that such power as she might attain would come to her by way of a man. Wallis had no job or career of her own, and it was apparent that her best chance for bettering her social and financial position would be via marriage.

Thus far, the astrologer reasoned well. When he predicted "substantial" power for Wallis, though, common sense let him down. Wallis came awfully close to power. She was engaged to marry King Edward VIII and fully expected to be crowned Queen of England. In the end, though, the British people would not stand for their king marrying a twice-divorced woman. Edward was forced to abdicate, and Wallis's chance at "power" slipped away.

Jeane Dixon's predictions also display a broad streak of common sense. Among her forecasts for late 1985 and early 1986 was a suggestion that Elizabeth Taylor would soon experience "her next great love." This seemed likely, considering the actress's past history of almost nonstop romance. Common sense also appears to have guided Dixon when she predicted that Taylor's "struggle against alcohol and drugs will be difficult, but not as difficult as the struggle to stay slim." As most people know, Elizabeth Taylor has been hospitalized with a drug and alcohol abuse problem and has waged a long battle against overweight.

Common sense also helps when it comes to predicting disaster. Followers of Edgar Cayce, the Sleeping Prophet, point out that he successfully predicted earthquakes, volcanoes, tidal waves, and storms in and around the Pacific Ocean. Skeptics respond that the Pacific is a notoriously active earthquake and volcano zone and that typhoons and other violent storms strike the area regularly. In fact, disasters, both natural and man-made, are so frequent in nearly every part of the globe that prophets are usually safe in predicting them, especially if they keep their forecasts general. The year 1985 was particularly rich in catastrophe. Scores drowned when a dam burst in Italy; mud slides in Puerto Rico killed hundreds more; earthquakes devastated parts of Mexico and the Soviet Union; forest fires flamed across the American West; and hurricanes swept up the East Coast and across the Gulf States. A volcanic eruption in South America claimed over 23,000 lives. On just one day in October, there was an earthquake in New York, a killer typhoon in the Philippines, and deadly monsoon storms in India. Add to all that the fact that 1985 was the worst-ever year for airplane crashes—nearly 2,000 died—and it's clear that anyone who forecast disaster for that year was almost sure to have been right on target.

So far in this chapter, we have looked at how predictions can be fulfilled, more or less, because of the knowledge, experience, or common sense of

*Early in the morning of September 19, 1985, a powerful earthquake struck Mexico. This was just one of many disasters that occurred that year, a year in which anyone who predicted natural or man-made devastation stood a good chance of being right.* (REUTERS / BETTMANN NEWSPHOTOS)

the prophet. They can come true, or can seem to come true, for other reasons, too. One of the biggest is that people want them to.

Human beings have a powerful need to try to see into the future. In order for that need to be satisfied, they must believe that accurate prediction is possible, and in order to believe that, they must feel that correct forecasts have been made in the past. However, their eagerness to believe sometimes leads people to accept as true predictions of questionable value.

Questionable prophecies often show up in the world's folklore. Could King Enmenduranna really see into the future? Did an ancient Sumerian really predict a great flood? The people of long-ago times accepted both legends as fact, just as, centuries later, the English accepted the tales about the prophecies of Mother Shipton. Successful prophecies are also part of religious lore and tradition. The Christian and Jewish Bibles contain many examples, and so do the holy writings of other faiths. Millions of people believe in the literal truth of these prophecies, while others regard them as symbolic or allegorical.

More modern predictions may also win acceptance from many, even when their reliability is decidedly unproven. Again, many accept them because of their determination to believe that the future is knowable.

Sometimes that determination takes the form of a reluctance to look very hard at the claims a prophet makes. Did Jeane Dixon truly warn President Roosevelt in November 1945 that he had only six months to live? No biography of Roosevelt mentions any visit Dixon ever paid to him. Roosevelt's secretary denied ever making an appointment for a visit, and so did his administrative assistant. The assistant did say that Dixon told her that she was at the White House, but she did not claim to have seen Jeane Dixon there herself. (Incidentally, Dixon and the assistant were close personal friends.) The Secret Service, charged with protecting the president at all times, has no record of Dixon's coming to see Roosevelt.

One person, Roosevelt's son Elliot, has said he recalls that his father referred to talking with Jeane Dixon. However, since Elliot does not profess to have been present at the meeting between the two, he cannot act as witness to whatever Dixon may have had to say. Dixon's claim to have predicted Roosevelt's death rests upon her word alone. Yet thousands accept that claim. In the same way, thousands are willing to believe in prophetic dreams and visions, even when there is little or no independent evidence that such dreams and visions ever took place.

Another tactic that would-be believers may employ is that of searching through history and ferreting out events that seem to fit the conditions of earlier predictions. This practice has done much to enhance the reputation of Nostradamus.

Nostradamus says in *Century II*:

"Near the harbor and in two cities,
Will be two scourges the like of which have never been seen.
Hunger plague within, people thrown out by the sword
Will cry for help from the great immortal God."

Erika Cheetham, an English author who has written about Nostradamus, maintains that this passage refers to the dropping of nuclear bombs on Hiroshima and Nagasaki. To her, "plague" is the radiation sickness suffered by those exposed to the fallout from the bombs, and "the sword" means war in general. She regards the phrase, "near the harbor and in two cities," as identifying the two Japanese seacoast towns. The scourge that had never been seen before was, of course, the atomic bomb, which the world first heard about at the moment Hiroshima felt its awesome power.

But wait a minute! The world has thousands of harbor cities. Ocean harbors, lake harbors, river harbors. And why only one harbor? Hiroshima and Nagasaki are on separate islands, at different harbors two hundred miles apart. What kind of scourges? Why two distinct ones? The same type of weapon was used against both cities. Granted, a person can interpret Nostradamus's verse in a way that seems to fit the bombings. But it could probably be made to fit a number of other events equally well.

As a matter of fact, some of Nostradamus's predictions *have* been read as referring to one place or event, then, as a "better fit" comes along, to another. One verse that has undergone this process is also from *Century II*: *"Plus part du champ encontre Hister sera . . . Quand rien enfant de Germain observera."* Cheetham translates this as, "The greater part of the battlefield will be against Hitler. . . . When the child of Germany observes no law." As she points out, though, before the 1930s, when Hitler rose to prominence, "Hister" was accepted as meaning the Danube River, known in ancient times as the Ister. Then Hitler arrived on the scene, a personality who matched the rhyme so neatly that believers gave it a whole new meaning.

That is, Hitler is a neat match for anyone willing to ignore the discrepancy in spelling between "Hister" and "Hitler" and to set aside the jarring reality that Hitler was born in Austria, not Germany. But disregarding the facts, or even twisting and distorting them, is not unheard of among those bent on proving the accuracy of this or that prediction.

One early twentieth-century French clairvoyant, for instance, is said to have predicted the outbreak of World War I with these words, "The future of Belgium is extraordinarily sad. . . . This land will set all Europe in flames." The prediction was made in 1905, nine years before the war began.

To accept it as a true vision of coming events is to set history on its head. Belgium did not *set* Europe in flames; it *was set* in flames by German troops when they invaded that small neutral country in August 1914. Belgium did not start the war, as the prediction implies; it was the war's innocent victim. True, sad events awaited Belgium in 1905, but they also awaited every other nation fated to participate in the slaughter of world war: England, France, Germany, Luxembourg, Montenegro, Japan, Russia, Serbia, Turkey, Austria-Hungary, Bulgaria, Poland, Italy, Portugal, Rumania, Greece, and the United States.

So eager are a few to demonstrate that they, or others, can see into the future that they do not stop at twisting historical facts. They are prepared to step in and try to direct events in order that a prediction may be fulfilled.

One who did this was the self-proclaimed son of Nostradamus, a man who called himself Michel le jeune (Michel the younger). In 1574, Michel was present at the siege of the French town of Poussin. Asked what the outcome of the siege would be, he predicted that Poussin would burn to the ground. Soon after, French soldiers discovered Michel sneaking around the city walls and setting fire to them. He was executed on the spot.

But of all who have sought to mold events to prophecy, the person who must get credit for resorting to the most extreme measures is Geronimo Cardano. Cardano was the Italian astrologer who predicted that King Edward VI of England would fall mortally ill at age fifty-five when, in fact, Edward died before he was seventeen. Undaunted by this, Cardano was bold enough to announce that he himself would die when he was seventy-five. Imagine his dismay when his seventy-fifth birthday came and went, leaving him as hale and hearty as ever. Cardano, so his friends said, took his own life to prove the stars correct.

The frauds perpetrated by Cardano and Michel le jeune were responses to the failure of predictions to come true. Other frauds of prophecy have been designed from the start to be deceptions. Several prophecies attributed to Mother Shipton, including those quoted in Chapter 2, have been revealed as nineteenth-century forgeries. Nostradamus forgeries, many of them prepared by politicians hopeful of seeming destined to succeed and of making their rivals seem destined to fail, began appearing as long ago as the mid-seventeenth century.

Twentieth-century politicians have also used Nostradamus counterfeits to gain their ends. Adolf Hitler ordered verses, written in the prophet's distinctive style, that predicted a German triumph in World War II. These were scattered from airplanes flying over parts of France in the early 1940s. The Allied forces fighting against Hitler responded with Nostradamus forgeries of their own that predicted Allied victory.

Hitler may also have used Nostradamus to bolster his popularity at home. Remember the prediction that Hitler claimed saved his life in 1939, the one that supposedly warned him of an assassination plot directed against him in Munich? In Hitler's account, his official astrologer based his prediction upon a verse in *Century VI*:

"The people are assembled . . .
Princes and kings among many bystanders.
The pillars, the walls fall, but as if by a miracle
The King . . . [is] saved."

But was this verse used to predict the Munich bombing—or to plan it? Many historians believe it was the latter. Hitler, they say, engineered the incident to make it seem that he had been in danger and to win sympathy for his cause. The stage was set carefully: the onlookers, the top Nazi party leaders, the pillars behind the rostrum from which Hitler addressed the crowd, the falling walls, and, most essential of all, the "King's" seemingly miraculous escape minutes before the bomb went off. All was arranged to correspond to the prophecy.

Fakery, forgery, and false interpretation at worst; common sense, experience, and social and political awareness at best—is that all that lies behind those prophecies and predictions that appear to have been inspired by some mystical or supernatural force?

If it is, how do we explain the prophetic visions of Joan of Arc?

How do we explain Nostradamus's prediction that London would burn in "three times twenty plus six"?

Or that King Henri II was doomed to a terrible death, his eye pierced in its "cage of gold"? In that prophecy, Nostradamus even included the precise—and accurate—detail that the king would be killed by someone younger than himself: "The young lion will overcome the old one."

If mystic prophecy is explainable only as trickery or as knowledge and common sense, what of Abraham Lincoln's dream, the one in which he was told he would be shot by an assassin?

What of Gerard Croiset, Sr., credited by the police of more than one country with helping them solve crimes?

Or of his son, who "saw" the details of the 1972 Uruguayan plane crash in the Andes Mountains? Although some of the details Gerard, Jr., provided were wrong—he had said that the plane was in or near a lake, for instance, and it was not—he gave the families at least one valuable hint that could have been used to locate the wreck. In Croiset's vision, the aircraft seemed to be lying in a spot forty-one miles south of the mountain pass of Planchon in Chile. Actually, it was forty-one miles *north* of Planchon.

Anyone who denies the ability of mystics to penetrate the mists of time to come should consider the prediction made in 1915 by Edith Lyttelton, an Englishwoman and a Dame of the British Empire. Dame Edith's prophecy was revealed through automatic writing, in which a person in a trance allows a pen to move freely over a piece of paper.

"The nemesis of Fate nearer and nearer—" Dame Edith wrote dreamily. " . . . the leaves of the autumn . . . the price of peace. . . . The Munich bond remember that . . . "

Twenty-four years later, remembering the Munich bond was exactly what people around the world were doing. A year before, in 1938, Adolf Hitler had announced plans to march into Czechoslovakia and seize a chunk of it. England and France, although obliged by treaty to defend Czech rights, hesitated to do so. Instead, leaders of those two nations met with Hitler in Munich to sign a pact allowing Germany to take the territory.

To British Prime Minister Neville Chamberlain, the Munich Pact was a victory. "Peace in our time," he said. The price of that peace would be high, Chamberlain's critics predicted. The Munich Pact would only encourage Hitler to think he could get away with more. They were right. World War II began in September 1939, when the German dictator attempted to repeat in Poland what he had gotten away with in Czechoslovakia.

Five years later, a series of strangely prophetic words appeared in a London *Daily Telegraph* crossword puzzle. What, other than some parapsychological phenomenon, can explain them?

The words, all of which appeared in puzzles published between May 23 and June 2, 1944, were Overlord, Utah, Omaha, Neptune, and Mulberry. Top British intelligence agents read them and shuddered. The agents were among the tiny handful of people who knew that Allied commanders had given the word for a June 6 invasion of German-occupied France. The planned invasion was known by the code name of Operation Overlord. It called for naval operations—code-named Neptune—to get underway from artificial harbors—code-named Mulberry—secured off two French beaches code-named Omaha and Utah.

Aghast at the apparent lapse in security and appalled at the thought that German spies might be at work, the agents arrested the man who had written the puzzles and questioned him closely. His answers eventually satisfied them. He was no spy, and there had been no leak of military information. How, then, had the prophetic words come into his mind? How else than by ESP?

How else did Jeane Dixon sense, in 1952, that a Democrat would be elected president in 1960 and that he would be assassinated? This is a Dixon prediction vouched for by an outsider, nationally known newspaper columnist Jack Anderson. Anderson quotes an article he wrote for the May 13, 1956, issue of *Parade* magazine. "As for the 1960 election, Mrs. Dixon thinks it will be won by a Democrat, but he will be assassinated or die in office." Can any rationalist explain that?

Many would try. Sir Francis Bacon, the seventeenth-century English thinker and writer, might have pointed out that this prophecy, and others whose accuracy seems unquestionable, are the exception, rather than the rule. Accurate mystic predictions represent only a tiny number picked from among thousands of false ones. Yet they are the ones people remember. "Men mark when they [astrologers and other prophets] hit, and never mark when they miss," Sir Francis wrote. The eighteenth-century French writer François Voltaire expressed himself even more cynically. No prophet, he said, "should claim the exclusive privilege of being wrong all the time."

Still, the suspicion lingers that there is more here than appears on the surface, that there is much we humans do not know about time past and time to come, and about the special ability some may have to peer into those times. At a 1972 meeting of the Parapsychological Association in Scotland, Dr. Russell Targ of California's Stanford Research Institute suggested that time may not always flow in a simple forward direction. Many happenings produce strong effects after their occurrence, he noted. Wars, assassinations, and natural catastrophes are examples. Perhaps, Targ went on, some happenings are unsettling enough to produce a *weak* effect *before* they occur. Such effects might be recognized by a person with parapsychological powers.

Others consider Targ's idea—or similar time warp theories—worth thinking about. Parapsychologists at the University of Utrecht in the Netherlands have investigated some of the possibilities with the two Croisets and with other gifted mediums. In the United States, psychologist J. B. Rhine did the same at Duke University.

Scientists working at Dr. Rhine's laboratory demonstrated that some people do possess an unusual ability to predict certain events. Experiments have shown conclusively that some excel at guessing the shapes of symbols printed on cards they cannot see. Of course, anyone will guess the shapes correctly once in a while. The laws of probability dictate that. But a few of those tested at Duke and elsewhere accurately predicted the shapes much more often than probability theory can explain. Other respected twentieth-century scholars and thinkers who have believed in the existence of pre-cognition include the English writers J. B. Priestley and Arthur Koestler.

And why not? Couldn't there be something, some force, some power, some mysterious energy, that allows those sensitive to it to read the future before it unfolds? Couldn't the mystic prophets of past and present have learned to tap into some source of knowledge that they—and we—do not yet understand?

Perhaps. Once, people did not know about or understand electricity, although they could plainly see some of its effects in the world around them. Eventually, over the years, they learned to harness this great force and make it work for them. We humans have learned to recognize other, once inexplicable, natural forces, too, forces such as nuclear energy and magnetism, and bend them to our use. Maybe we will one day do the same with pre-ternatural parapsychological forces. Maybe we will find scientific explanations for such forces, explanations that will convince even the most rational among us that accurate prophecy can spring from mystic sources.

After all, that's what happened when science finally accepted the fact that catfish can predict earthquakes.

F · I · V · E

# How Dependable a Science?

**F**ar beneath the islands of Japan there lives a giant catfish. The creature is usually quiet, but sometimes it begins to wriggle about. When it does—earthquake! Generations of Japanese parents have told this story to their children. Probably only the youngest really believed it.

But even the oldest and wisest Japanese believed another "fish story." By observing the behavior of catfish, they claimed, they could predict a coming quake. When the fish begin acting skittery, swimming erratically and leaping out of the water, an earthquake is about to strike.

Meaningless folklore? For years, scientists maintained that it was. Then, during the 1930s, experiments by a Japanese researcher suggested that catfish may be sensitive to weak electrical signals in water. Suppose, just before an earthquake, those signals change slightly. Then the fish, sensing the change, would grow jumpy.

Later experiments by American scientists confirmed that catfish—and some other animals—do sometimes exhibit abnormal behavior just before a quake. The scientists are not sure why. Electrical changes may be the answer. Or it may be because of alterations in the earth's magnetic field or because of the very high-pitched sounds given off by rocks under the enormous strains that precipitate a tremor. Animals can hear such sounds, but people cannot.

Whatever the reason, it is clear that this ancient method of earthquake prediction—once dismissed as superstitious nonsense—can work. The fish do respond to some as yet unknown force that warns them of disaster to come. Geologists and other scientists accept this as fact today. Parapsychologists might say that the scientists should go a step further and accept the idea that they will one day discover rational scientific explanations for some of the other methods mystics use to predict the future.

But even if we do eventually find that the mysteries of prophecy can be accounted for by science, isn't parapsychological prediction just too uncertain to rely upon? Even most of those who are convinced that mystics can occasionally catch a genuine glimpse of the future admit that such glimpses are few and far between. Wouldn't it be better, for the practical purpose of preparing and planning for the future, to trust to the predictions of science?

Many think so. Certainly it was scientists, not catfish-watchers, who predicted the 1975 earthquake in Haicheng, China. Acting on the scientists' advice, Chinese officials ordered the city evacuated. Thousands of lives were saved.

The next year, though, it was a different story for the scientists of China. Early in the morning of July 28, 1976, the earth began shaking in Tangshan, three hundred miles southwest of Haicheng. Minutes later, 800,000 men, women, and children were dead. Geologists, all their knowledge about plate tectonics and earthquake prediction notwithstanding, had not suspected that disaster was imminent. The quake that killed over 7,000 people in Mexico in September 1985 and the one that shook up the New York City area the next month also went unpredicted by science.

These are not the only examples of failure in scientific prediction. Weather forecasters have a particularly poor reputation. With all their maps and charts and instruments and satellites and photography and imaging and computers, meteorologists still seem to get the picture wrong a fair bit of the time.

One time came in November 1980. On the twenty-first of that month, three Massachusetts lobstermen checked the National Weather Service forecast for the Georges Bank. Located in the stormy North Atlantic, the Georges Bank is known equally for its rich fishing grounds and its tempestuous weather. This time, though, the forecast was favorable. Good weather and calm seas lay ahead, Weather Service forecasters said. The lobstermen set sail from Cape Cod.

They never returned. On November 22, a storm unexpectedly blew up.

The men and their boat vanished in hundred-mile-an-hour winds and sixty-foot waves. Four years later, a judge in Boston ruled that the faulty prediction made the Weather Service and its parent organization, the National Oceanographic and Atmospheric Administration (NOAA), liable for the men's deaths. The next August, he ordered them to pay the families $1.25 million in damages.

The predictions of weather forecasters are based upon their observations of the earth and its atmosphere. Beyond the atmosphere lies the void of space—realm of the predictions of astronomy. So regular are the movements of stars, planets, comets, and other heavenly bodies that astronomers are able to predict their risings and settings, comings and goings, with complete accuracy. Yet astronomers are not infallible. Early in 1973, they were predicting a space spectacular for late that year, the comet Kahoutec. Kahoutec would be visible to the naked eye, its great tail a sight to see and remember forever, the scientists said. But they were wrong. Kahoutec could barely be seen through strong binoculars. "A disappointment," one United States astronomer termed it.

Prophets in other fields of science occasionally miss the mark, too. Pollsters claim that their methods are strictly scientific, yet their predictions are not always accurate or even consistent. Before the 1984 presidential election, for instance, virtually every pollster in the country forecast that President Ronald Reagan would defeat his challenger, Walter Mondale. The pollsters were correct. Reagan won by 52 million votes to 36 million. With 59 percent of the electorate on his side, compared to only 41 percent for Mondale, Reagan enjoyed an eighteen percentage point advantage over his rival.

But accurate as the polls were about the winner, several turned out to be less reliable about the percentage-point spread between the two candidates. The Gallup poll, perhaps the nation's best known, got it just right. A poll conducted jointly by the *New York Times* and CBS-TV came close—22 percent—and so did *The Washington Post*–ABC-TV poll—14 percent. For a poll's results to be off by three or four percentage points is not unusual. According to the laws of probability, upon which polling is based, a certain degree of error is unavoidable.

But not the degree of error displayed in the 1984 polls. A survey conducted by NBC-TV showed Reagan winning by twenty-four percentage points, and one by the newspaper *USA Today* gave him a twenty-five point edge. By contrast, the Louis Harris poll and a poll taken by the Roper Organization—both reputable companies—predicted that the president would have no more than a ten- or eleven-point lead.

The techniques of political polling are applied to other areas of public opinion research, and there, too, mistakes can occur. One stunning example came in the field of commercial market research.

In April 1985, the Coca-Cola Company announced it was changing its ninety-nine-year-old soft drink formula. Two years of extensive research had demonstrated that consumers would prefer a sweeter taste in the future, company officials declared. The old formula would be "retired," buried forever in the depths of a bank vault.

Three months later, red-faced Coke officials were gulping their words. "New Coke" was a bust. Across the country, consumers were up in arms, demanding a return to the familiar taste. Back came the original formula, now dubbed "Coke Classic." By fall, it was outselling the new, market-researched Coke by a margin of nine to one.

Predictions can go awry in other business areas. In 1980, many economists were prophesying good times ahead. Instead, the United States fell into a serious economic slump, the worst recession since the Great Depression of the 1930s. Business did poorly, and hundreds of thousands of working men and women lost their jobs. Many also lost their homes, while others, unable to keep up with credit-card payments, lost autos or appliances or went into bankruptcy. Two years later, it was good times that the economists failed to predict. By early 1985, the gross national product—the sum total of all goods and services produced around the nation—was growing at a yearly rate of over 10 percent, more than twice what the experts had predicted.

Industry has its prognosticators—and its mistaken prognostications—as well. Back in the 1950s and 1960s, scientists were predicting a glorious future for the nation's infant nuclear power industry. It wouldn't be long before nuclear power plants would be producing all the electrical energy Americans could use, they said. This electricity would be generated neatly, cleanly, and safely. There would be none of the mess and dirt of coal or the inconvenience of oil, much of which had to be imported from far-off lands. What was more, nuclear energy would be cheap—"too cheap to meter." That was the way the nuclear future looked to science thirty years ago.

It didn't turn out like that. Nuclear energy is expensive and getting more so. Plants that were supposed to cost $700 or $800 million to build are now costing $2 or $3 billion. Even when a plant is on line and producing electricity, it must be shut down regularly for safety checks and routine maintenance. Shutdowns are costly, and the prices consumers must pay have soared. Nuclear power isn't as safe as it was expected to be, either, as accidents have shown. The worst accident in the United States, so far, which took place at the Three Mile Island plant in Middletown, Pennsylvania, in 1979, brought the nation face to face with the threat of a nuclear meltdown and the radioactive contamination of hundreds of square miles. A Soviet nuclear power plant mishap in 1986 spread potentially hazardous radiation over much of Europe. Another problem that the early nuclear scientists failed to predict is that of deciding how to handle used nuclear fuel and old, worn-out plant parts. Today, thousands of tons of highly radioactive nuclear waste lie in temporary storage around the country. No one knows how to store the waste permanently and safely. No one even knows if safe, permanent storage is possible.

Other industries have experienced similar troubles with prediction. Scientists who work in the chemical industry, for instance, once promised farmers a future of powerful and effective pesticides and fertilizers. They offered consumers the advantages of efficient detergents and indestructible plastics. Faithfully, the industry fulfilled those pledges. But along with the new products came the unexpected: toxic waste. Dumped, often illegally, in every state in the union, poisonous chemicals have made whole neighborhoods—whole towns, even—unfit for humans to live in. They threaten animal life, too, as well as the air we breathe, the water we drink, and the land that produces the food we eat.

Why? What has gone wrong? With all the precise and sophisticated tools of modern science, why can't our scientific forecasters paint a clearer picture of what the future holds?

One set of answers has to do with the methods and procedures scientists use in making their predictions. If those methods and procedures are inadequate, the predictions will be inadequate as well.

Take the meteorologists who forecast fair weather on the Georges Bank for November 22, 1980. Their prediction was based on information gathered from earth-orbiting satellites, from aircraft passing over the area and ships sailing through it, from a ground network of weather observation posts, and from instruments mounted on buoys anchored far out at sea. Weather Service buoys are equipped to measure wind speed, air pressure, air and water temperatures, and wave height.

On November 21, however, one of two anemometers on a Weather Service buoy near the Georges Bank was not working properly. For two and a half months, it had been giving forecasters erratic wind-speed measurements. Because of this, the forecasters had decided to disregard all anemometer readings from that particular buoy. But their forecasts had included no warning to that effect.

The judge who found the Weather Service and NOAA responsible for the lobstermen's deaths cited that lack of warning as one reason for his ruling. He also criticized weather officials for permitting the anemometer to go unrepaired for so long. Sloppy methods and procedures had led to a false prediction and a tragic ending. That, at least, was the judge's verdict.

Inadequate techniques can help explain other errors of scientific prediction. Geologists who try to predict earthquakes or volcanoes, for example, may simply not yet know enough about plate tectonics to make exact prediction possible. As their knowledge grows, so may their ability to foretell future disasters. The same is true of doctors, who do not understand the causes of all diseases, nor always know the best ways to treat them. It can also be the case with astronomers, who must make calculations based on measurements of tiny amounts of light coming from hundreds of light-years away. Even in the late twentieth century, the tools and techniques in many areas of science are not up to making accurate prediction a certainty.

Inadequate or faulty techniques can underlie market research mistakes, too. Trying to explain the "New Coke" fiasco, Coca-Cola executives pointed out that in two whole years of research on nearly a quarter of a million consumers, analysts had failed to consider one vital issue. They had questioned Coke drinkers in depth about their reactions to the taste of the "New Coke." They had asked them how they liked it compared to the "old Coke." But never did they bother to ask people whether they would like to see *both* Cokes on supermarket shelves. They never even thought to warn the samples they talked with that if the company decided to go with the new formula, the old one might be scrapped. "That's bad research," one New York market analyst commented.

Methodology can also affect the reliability of political poll results. Many leading pollsters believe it may account for the discrepancies in the presidential election polls of 1984.

The most essential single ingredient in a successful political poll is a random sample. Without that, no poll can claim to be scientific in any way. But once a pollster does have a scientifically selected sample, the way in which he or she frames questions and asks them becomes the most important factor.

The wording of questions can incline members of a sample to answer in a particular way. "Do you approve of President Reagan's business policies?" and, "Do you approve of President Reagan's economic policies?" may sound a lot alike, but the two questions could elicit quite different answers. The word *business* may remind people that Reagan often seems to favor the needs of big business over those of labor unions and working men and women, while *economic* may make them think of the prosperous economy of 1984 and 1985. If Pollster A uses the first question, and Pollster B uses the second, A may find a lower approval rating for the president than B does. That could make a difference when the two begin to make predictions about vote spreads.

Even the order in which questions are asked—the most important one first? last? in the middle?—can alter results, some pollsters maintain. Another factor is the "undecideds." If a person in a sample says she's not sure how she's going to vote, or how she feels about an issue, should the researcher push her to make up her mind? Some pollsters say yes; others, no.

The manner in which a pollster approaches the sample may also have an effect. Some do it in person. Results are better that way, they say, because the researcher gets to make personal contact with each individual. Others prefer to use the telephone. It's more neutral, they believe, since it reduces the possibility that the researcher will influence a person's responses by a smile or a frown, or by some other, more subtle reaction.

Would a pollster do that? Aren't public opinion researchers trained never to display a reaction to the responses of the people they question?

Of course. But researchers are human, too, and like the rest of us, they have their own feelings, beliefs, and convictions, their own political, religious, and moral points of view. It is only to be expected that they will occasionally allow those convictions and points of view to creep in between themselves and their predictions. And that brings us to the second big reason that scientific prediction sometimes fails: the human factor.

It's easy to spot the human factor in political polls. The type of contact established, the wording and order of questions, the way "undecideds" are treated—all are the result of human judgment, and all can affect poll results. Independent pollsters try to take such variables into account and to neutralize them in order to produce the most objective findings possible. Even they, however, admit that they cannot eliminate the human factor entirely.

Other pollsters may not even attempt to. Among them are some of the researchers who work exclusively for a particular political party or group, or for an individual candidate for political office.

In no way can these researchers approach their work neutrally or objectively. Their job, like any political pollster's, is to find out how voters feel about the candidate and the issues. As the paid employees of a group or candidate, however, they have a stake in those findings—and a motive for trying to improve "their" candidate's chances in the next election. With all the variables that can affect even the most independent poll, how can politically committed pollsters hope to make predictions that are free of bias?

Other predictions that are supposed to be purely rational and scientific can be infected by human feelings, political or otherwise. After the Coke fiasco of 1985, company officials acknowledged that the idea of introducing a sweeter taste had been tied to their desire to boost Coke sales dramatically with a bold marketing move. Perhaps this desire blinded them to the faulty methodology in the test marketing of their new product.

A feeling of pride can color a forecast—and moderate its accuracy. An astronomer's ambition to be the first to predict an unusual celestial event might lead to a faulty prediction. An economist's commitment to a money theory he himself has developed could keep him from predicting problems that may come up if that theory is put into action. Wishing to win a place in medical history, a doctor may predict, prematurely, that she has discovered a new treatment that will eliminate a dreaded disease.

Fear is another powerful motive for making predictions. It is fear that makes many scientists predict environmental disaster unless toxic waste sites are cleaned up at once. Fear may play a part in scientists' predictions of such natural disasters as earthquakes and volcanoes, too.

Yet such predictions are also grounded in hope, the hope that lives and property can be saved if the warnings come in time. This is the hope that was fulfilled so brilliantly in Haicheng, China, in 1975. It is the hope that failed a year later in Tangshan.

Hope that the United States could free itself from a dependency on expensive foreign oil helped fuel the optimistic nuclear power industry's forecasts of twenty or thirty years ago. At the same time, those forecasts may have owed something to a less attractive human emotion, greed. Some of those responsible for the predictions either worked for or owned companies that stood to profit substantially if the new industry were successful.

Greed, hope, fear, political and social beliefs—these are just a few of the emotions that can get mixed up with predictions. Altogether, they add up to a human factor of tremendous proportions, a human factor that can stand in the way of science's best efforts to give us reliable, dependable forecasts for the future. And there is still another reason for the fact that even the most "scientific" of predictions are sometimes mistaken. Some events are just not predictable.

The storm that killed the three Massachusetts lobstermen in 1980 may have been such an event. According to many, the Boston judge erred in blaming the National Weather Service and NOAA for failing to predict the tempest. "It is doubtful that reliable wind data from the buoy in question would have made a tad of difference to the forecast," wrote Robert C. Cowen, natural science editor of the *Christian Science Monitor* after the verdict came down. The reason: Two low-pressure systems suddenly and unexpectedly met over the Georges Bank. A hurricanelike storm developed. "Computer-generated forecasts," Cowen went on, " . . . cannot anticipate such swift emergence of this kind of storm." In other words, the gale may have been unpredictable. A United States Appeals Court reflected this point of view when it overturned the $1.25 million award to the lobstermen's families. The families plan an appeal to the United States Supreme Court.

Other events are unpredictable. If, a week before an election, a news reporter reveals that the leading candidate lied about his war record—he falsely claimed to have won a hero's medal—the contest becomes unpredictable. Before the revelation, the lying candidate seemed sure to win. Now his lie will cause many voters to turn against him. But how many? And how many voters will vote for him anyway, feeling he's already suffered enough, or that everyone lies a little sometimes? No one can predict.

The factor that makes something unpredictable can be a new invention or a new technology. By the mid-1980s, researchers at the A. C. Nielsen Company and other businesses that measure television viewing patterns were finding it more and more difficult to predict viewer trends. Why? More channels were available than ever before, thanks to cable networks and to satellite-dish antennas. People were switching around from station to station and forgetting to tell researchers all the programs they watched each week. Besides that, VCRs were confusing the picture. People were recording one program while watching another. That, too, was being overlooked.

Economics is another field in which the unpredictable can happen. Business is booming, stock market investors are making money—and suddenly a company that seemed to be flourishing announces it is bankrupt. Stock market prices fall, and investors lose money. But losses can turn to gains just as unexpectedly, as two faltering companies announce plans to merge into one new, financially stronger corporation.

*Automated buoys such as the one this painting depicts collect weather data at sea and transmit it to forecasters at the United States Weather Service.* (NOAA)

Unpredictability may have played a role in the Coca-Cola Company's 1985 problems. Certainly, market researchers were careless not to have questioned consumers about the planned retirement of the original formula. But even if they had, they might not have learned all they needed to know. After the whole affair was over, some analysts suggested that consumers themselves might not have been aware of the depth of their feelings about Coke. Once the old taste was gone, that feeling surfaced. "People felt Coca-Cola represented Americana, and they don't want Americana to change on them," said one old Coke enthusiast. "It [Coke] has become part of the culture," a public opinion researcher from Chicago explained. A psychologist was more specific. Coke is "associated . . . with peace, happiness, winning, love, the essence of existence," he told reporters. Whatever the reason for the public's reaction, that reaction was there. "Something that just flat caught us by surprise," said Coca-Cola president Donald R. Keough. Something that just plain couldn't be predicted, perhaps.

But if the science of prediction fails upon occasion, it succeeds a great deal of the time. Few would deny that the tools and methods of science have transformed the ancient art of prophecy. And yet, just as scientific prediction can fail, inspired prediction can succeed. Sometimes, the two kinds succeed—or fail—for very similar reasons.

Scientific forecasters enjoy their greatest triumphs when they work painstakingly and objectively, observing phenomena accurately and ana-lyzing it unemotionally. When scientists become careless, or when they allow their personal feelings, beliefs, or prejudices to affect their outlook, their predictions are more likely to go astray.

It's not so different with mystics. Knowledge, experience, honesty, and an open mind are the best tools any prophet can have.

S · I · X

# The Perils
# of Prediction

The earthquakes started in 1978. Week after week, for four years, mild tremors shook the streets, stores, and homes of Mammoth Lakes, California. No one in town paid much attention. "Californians aren't afraid of earthquakes," one resident commented.

Even Californians, though, may feel apprehensive about volcanoes. When, in 1982, scientists at the United States Geological Survey announced that an underground reservoir of molten rock was moving toward the earth's surface just outside town, the people of Mammoth Lakes became alarmed. Then the geologists issued a volcano hazard alert for the mountain ski resort, and alarm changed to fear for many.

Between 1982 and 1984, the town's population dropped from over 5,000 to under 3,000. School enrollment slipped by 26 percent and new construction by 75 percent. Houses valued at $150,000 in 1982 were worth only $100,000 two years later.

Midway through 1984, the United States Geological Survey called off its alert. "Based on assessments of the current situation, a volcanic eruption does not pose an immediate threat to public safety," a spokesperson declared. But as far as the people of Mammoth Lakes were concerned, the damage had been done.

What happened in Mammoth Lakes could happen elsewhere. A few months after Geological Survey scientists canceled their volcano warning, they forecast a 1988 earthquake for Parkfield, about 150 miles southwest of Mammoth Lakes. Parkfield, with only thirty-four inhabitants, seemed unlikely to undergo the economic decline suffered by Mammoth Lakes. But the emotional upheaval for those living there could be much the same. It could be the same for people in many other places, too, as scientists become more confident of their ability to predict geological disasters—and more willing to do so. In the view of some, this uncertainty illustrates one of the problems with prophecy.

Predictions can create as many difficulties as they solve, the critics say. Just look at what happened in Haicheng, China, in 1975. Warned by geologists that an earthquake might be imminent, government authorities ordered the people of Haicheng to leave their homes, to abandon their vegetable plots and market stalls, to drop everything, and go into exile for an indefinite period of time. What if, after all that, the quake hadn't struck? What if the Chinese scientists had been as mistaken about Haicheng as the United States Geological Survey scientists apparently were about Mammoth Lakes? The dislocation would have been for nothing, just as the dislocation in Mammoth Lakes seems to have been.

But the Chinese weren't mistaken, others retort. They were right, and they saved hundreds, if not thousands, of lives. Better safe than sorry, they add, and that goes for Mammoth Lakes and Parkfield, too.

All right, the critics respond in their turn. Prediction served humanity well in Haicheng. But what about Tangshan, China, where 800,000 died in an unexpected quake a year and half later? Were the people of Tangshan lulled into a false sense of security by what had happened in Haicheng? Did they assume that if danger threatened, a warning would come in time to save them, too? If they did, prediction failed them. It failed the people of quake-torn Mexico City in 1985, as well, and the 23,000 or more who died in the eruption of Colombia's Nevado del Ruiz volcano a few weeks later. Yet scientists knew well in advance that an earthquake was very possible in Mexico, and, as we saw in Chapter 3, they had been monitoring hints of volcanic activity in Colombia throughout 1985. Why weren't warnings issued for those places, the critics demand, as they were for Mammoth Lakes and Parkfield? What use is scientific prediction if it warns of disasters that never happen and is silent about those that do occur?

The critics see other problems in prophecy. One is that people may put their trust in forecasts of dubious value.

The predictions of astrology are an example. Although astrologers claim that their art rests upon a foundation of science, scientists are vehement

64

in saying that this is not true. Astronomers disproved astrology's ancient assumptions about the stars and planets centuries ago. Nevertheless, millions of Americans profess to believe in astrology and in its ability to predict the future. That's not bad, astrology's detractors say, as long as they don't take horoscopes, sun signs, and all the rest of it too seriously. But when they do take it overly seriously, they could be risking their lives and happiness. Worse, they could risk the lives and happiness of others.

An astrological book on child-rearing, for example, suggested how parents might raise their children according to each child's sun sign. Much of what the book had to say was perfectly sound. The parents of children born under the sign of Cancer were told to cultivate a feeling of openness so that the children can feel free to discuss their feelings. Parents of a Gemini should give their child some listening time. Good advice. All parents should encourage communication within the family and spend time listening to their children.

But the parents of a Scorpio child are warned that their child may be sneaky or tyrannical, while an Aquarian child may be rebellious and precocious. A Libra takes indications of differing opinions as a personal rejection.

Telling parents how to deal with a sneaky child, or with one who is rebellious or very bright, or gets her feelings hurt easily is fine—if the child really is sly, disobedient, smart, or sensitive. But couldn't labeling a child one of these, particularly at an early age, do real damage? If a mother expects her son to turn out sneaky, isn't she likely to distrust him right from the start? A boy who's always being accused of lying and cheating when he isn't doing either seems likely to run into problems growing up. And pity the poor Aquarian of average intelligence. Will her parents regard her as lazy and defiant when Bs and Cs show up on her report card?

Astrological predictions are not the only ones that can be harmful if they are accepted too willingly and uncritically. Thirty years ago, most Americans believed those in the nuclear industry who assured them that the new energy source would be clean, safe, dependable, and cheap. Few stopped to consider that those predictions were coming from people who stood to profit from the technology. So the country embraced a future of nuclear power—a future that was to include accidents, spiraling costs, and an unsolved nuclear waste storage problem.

Another problem the critics point to is that predictions may be misused. One serious misuse occurred, they say, on Election Day 1980.

That day, Americans went to the polls to choose between Democratic

President Jimmy Carter, who was running for reelection, and his Republican rival, Ronald Reagan. Throughout the day, poll takers for the national television networks interviewed voters, asking them how they had cast their ballots. By the time the networks began their election reporting, at about 7:00 P.M. Eastern Standard Time, the trend was clear and surprising. The election had been expected to be very close; instead, a great majority of the interviewed voters had indicated that they supported Reagan. Excitedly, TV reporters began telling audiences the news: Ronald Reagan would win in a landslide.

But 7:00 P.M. in New York City is only late afternoon on the West Coast. There, people were hearing the predictions before many of them had even gotten a chance to vote. Thousands decided not to bother. West Coast Democrats, in particular, certain that their candidate had lost, stayed away from the voting booths. The result, political analysts agreed, was that several Democratic candidates lost congressional races that they might otherwise have won.

Not that the analysts accused the network reporters and executives of having had any political motivation for what they did. Their aim had not been to help Republican candidates, but to be the first to make a prediction. The networks may have acted carelessly, but they had not acted fraudulently. A different problem arises when people do use predictions in a conscious effort to manipulate people or events.

We've already seen how Adolf Hitler used—or abused—the prophecies of Nostradamus and the art of astrology. Others misuse predictions in a less blatant, but still unscrupulous fashion. Politicians may do so by commissioning polls with questions deliberately designed to elicit answers that will make them look more popular than they really are. Such politicians hope the polls will stir up public interest and enthusiasm, turning "undecideds" and even opponents into eager backers.

In the business world, too, predictions may be abused by people seeking only to profit. In 1985, one mail-order company that sells guns and survival equipment was trying to raise sales by quoting predictions about a rising American crime rate and the likelihood of race warfare in United States cities. Critics regard salesmanship of this kind as unethical.

Another problem is that some predictions can turn out to be self-fulfilling. That was one of the troubles with the television networks' 1980 election evening vote projections. By *predicting* Republican winners, the networks may have helped to *create* Republican winners.

Even in everyday life, we can see examples of self-fulfilling prophecies. If Maggie goes to a party in an I'm-going-to-have-a-lousy-time mood, chances are she will. If Sam's first-grade teacher puts him in the lowest reading group, that amounts to a prediction that he will never be much of a reader. If Sam accepts that prediction, he is not going to work hard to improve his reading skills. Odds are he'll stay in the bottom group.

A similar thing can happen with IQ scores or aptitude tests. Tell a student she has an IQ of 110 and a flair for history, and she will probably feel better about herself and more enthusiastic about studying than someone who believes her IQ is 90 and that she has no special aptitude. Actually both students may have IQs of 100—the average—and could do equally well in history. IQ and aptitude scores, like any test scores, can vary from time to time, depending on how a person is feeling and upon other factors. But the girl who expects to succeed in life may be better equipped to do just that than one who expects to be below average.

There is yet another problem some see in making predictions. This problem concerns the nature of the future and a debate that has been going on since men and women first walked this earth.

The debate is between those who believe that the future is predetermined and those who do not. Those in the first category say that every event has been ordained ahead of time and is unavoidable and inexorable. Those in the second believe that we humans have the freedom and the ability to influence events and to alter their course.

Many prophets, and those who trust in them, fall into the first group. Jeane Dixon, for instance, believes in predetermination, at least much of the time. When she prophesied John Kennedy's assassination, for example, she *knew* that the president's death had been willed by God. No warning, no human intervention, could have kept Lee Harvey Oswald from firing at Kennedy's motorcade as it passed through the streets of Dallas, Dixon maintains. From the beginning of time, Oswald's bullet was destined to pierce the president's skull, and nothing and no one could have stopped it.

Another Dixon prediction is that World War III will break out in 1999. Is this, too, inevitable?

Many think so. Nostradamus predicted it, and so did Edgar Cayce. Others believe the Bible foretells that war will come at century's end. The Book of Revelation, the last book of the New Testament, contains a powerful vision of the great final battle, the conflict that is to signal the end of the world and usher in the Day of Judgment:

"And he gathered them together into a place called . . . Armageddon.

" . . . and there was a great earthquake, such as was not since men were upon the earth, so mighty an earthquake, *and* so great . . .

"And every island fled away, and the mountains were not found.

"And there fell upon men a great hail out of heaven . . . and men blasphemed God because of the plague of the hail; for the plague thereof was exceeding great."

The plague, the hail, the total destruction, the quake unlike any ever known—do they describe the thundering explosions, the devastation of the land, the deadly radioactive fallout of a nuclear war? There are those who say they do. Even President Reagan has occasionally hinted at a belief in a not-too-distant nuclear Armageddon.

Mystics and religious visionaries are not alone in making nuclear pre-

*"Near the harbor and in two cities," Nostradamus wrote over 400 years ago, "will be two scourges the like of which have never been seen." Was the prophet predicting the 1945 devastation of the Japanese cities of Hiroshima (above) and Nagasaki by atomic bombs?* (UPI / BETTMANN NEWSPHOTOS)

dictions. Scientists, including the physicists and engineers who design and build this country's defensive and offensive weapons systems, make them, too. Their predictions concern the weapons themselves, the amount of damage each can do, the number that will be needed to counter any enemy threat, the best ways to distribute them at United States military bases around the globe, the way to protect them from sabotage or direct attack, and so on.

Other predictions come from the people who study and analyze our relations with other nations, particularly with the nation that many Americans think of as their main rival, the Soviet Union. Their predictions have to do with Soviet military and diplomatic goals, the likelihood that Soviet leaders will want to take on this country in battle, the way a nuclear war might begin, and the like. Still more predictions come from the men and women charged with devising strategy to protect Americans in the event of nuclear attack. These people work for the Federal Emergency Management Agency (FEMA). In general, their predictions are rosy. City dwellers will move to rural areas, food supplies will be shipped to the hungry and medicines to the sick and injured, mail will be delivered and taxes collected—such are the nuclear-war predictions of FEMA.

Less optimistic forecasts come from other scientists and from leaders and members of the nation's antinuclear groups and organizations. FEMA's postwar plans are nonsense, these people say. All-out nuclear war would be a war without winners. The holocaust would destroy earth's culture and most of its people. Great cities would burst into flame and crumble into dust. The countryside would be laid waste. Animals would perish; crops would not grow. Intense nuclear radiation would mean death for any who dared to venture outdoors. Clouds of smoke and dust—the unburied remains of our towns and cities, of our homes, schools, factories, and places of worship— would drift through the atmosphere choking out the sun's rays. Thus would dawn a "nuclear winter," an age of year-round freezing temperatures and raging blizzards. The desolation would be utter.

The nuclear winter prediction came in the early 1980s. Among the first to voice it was Carl Sagan, a United States astrophysicist and antinuclear activist. Sagan's is a grim prophecy. Grim, too, are the predictions of scientists and military experts who believe that nuclear war is probable, or even possible. So are the doom-laden visions presented to us by Jeane Dixon and other mystics. Even FEMA's hopeful outlook is hardly encouraging, since the agency's predictions are for a world that has already undergone nuclear war.

What happens if we in the world today accept such predictions as true—if we look upon the future as predetermined and nuclear conflagration and the destruction of our earth as inevitable? Will we then have any motive to try to avoid that fate, to work for peace and international understanding, to try to end the nuclear arms race?

If we, and our leaders, cannot believe in peace, surely we cannot have peace. If we are convinced that war must come, then come it must. And prophecy will have served us ill indeed.

## S·E·V·E·N

# The Promise of Prediction

The oldest recorded prophecy is a dream of peace. At first, though, it didn't seem that way.

To Gilgamesh, his dream appeared to foretell a final, fatal battle between himself and Enkidu, enemy of his people. Awakening, the Sumerian hero-king steeled himself to meet his own personal Armageddon.

But Ninsun was wiser than her son. Where there is the threat of war, she told him, there must also be the possibility of peace. Pursue the possibility, not the threat, Ninsun urged, and Gilgamesh followed her counsel. Enmity changed to friendship for the ancient peoples of Mesopotamia.

So it can be for us today. We, like Gilgamesh, have glimpsed terrifying visions of our future: A Biblical Armageddon, the great turn-of-the-millennium war envisioned by prophets and visionaries past and present, the nuclear conflagration scenarios worked out by government and military experts, the "nuclear winter" predictions of Carl Sagan and others. But if we are wise, like Ninsun, we will recognize that none of these is a vision of the future as it *must* be, but of the future as it *could* be. And, warned by the terrible "could," we, again like Ninsun, may seize the opportunity to act with resolution to ensure that that future never comes to pass.

That is the mission of those who would know the future. To inform us of the possibilities and offer us the chance to choose among them, that is their chief aim and highest purpose. It is what the best of our prophets, mystical and scientific, past and present, seek to give us. It is something

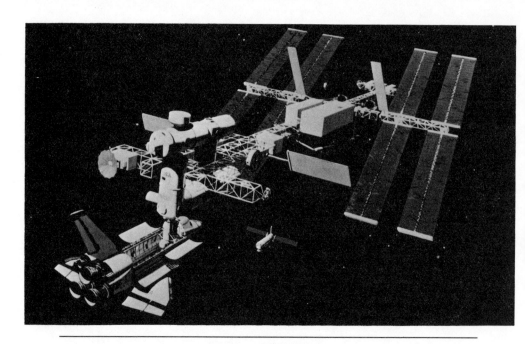

Will the United States have a permanent space station in orbit sometime during the 1990s? Many futurists believe the answer is yes. This space station model may be transformed into one that space pioneers of the future will call home. (NASA) An engineer inspects a "mock-up" of the interior of a space station command module. Testing and retesting the mock-up gives astronauts and space flight officials the opportunity to predict how well the space station's technology will operate when it is put into use. (NASA)

we of the dangerous and volatile late twentieth century need as much—
or more—than any who have lived before us.

One organization whose members attempt to fulfill that mission is the
World Future Society. Founded in 1967, the society describes itself as "dedicated
to the serious study of alternative future possibilities." Its findings are published in its regular bimonthly magazine, *The Futurist.* Among the topics
covered in recent issues: space stations and colonies, the future of computers,
unemployment in the twenty-first century, coming energy demands, and
education for the next generation. Helping people to understand what changes
the future may hold, says Edward S. Cornish, president of the group, will
allow them to prepare for those changes. Interest in the society's work is
high. In 1985, it had 3,000 members in eighty countries around the world.

Although the World Future Society is an educational, nonprofit-making
group, other futurist organizations are private income-producing businesses.
Forecasting International, of Arlington, Virginia, is an example. Headed by
Dr. Marvin Cetron, Forecasting International essays to reduce people's anx-
iety about the future. People are "getting scared," Cetron says, and not just
by talk about such horrors as the possibility of nuclear war. It is change
itself and the rapid pace of that change in the modern world that frighten
many, Cetron believes. To him, as to Edward Cornish, the goal of prediction
is to give people the opportunity to examine change ahead of time, before
it is thrust upon them.

Even the United States Congress has an institutionalized means of
looking into the future—the Congressional Clearinghouse on the Future.
Representative Robert W. Edgar of Pennsylvania serves as its chairman.

The Congressional Clearinghouse on the Future, like Forecasting International and the World Future Society, takes a rational, scientific approach
to the future. But mystics and visionaries also have institutions dedicated
to studying and utilizing their ancient arts. The Central Premonitions Registry, opened in London in January 1967, is an example. The next year,
a similar bureau was established in New York City. Both are devoted to
collecting, recording, and analyzing parapsychological visions and prophecies.

In its first year alone, the London Central Premonitions Registry received
500 predictions, nearly all of which concerned earthquakes, airplane crashes,
and other disasters. During the next year, thousands more poured in. Most
of them came from the same half-dozen or so men and women. According
to British writer Andrew MacKenzie, several turned out to correspond to

later real-life events. Erika Cheetham suggests that, in time, Premonitions Registries could develop into "advance warning systems, especially for natural disasters."

Both the mystic art of prophecy and the rational science of prediction are under study at colleges and universities in various parts of the world. While men and women in one laboratory press ahead with systematic research into parapsychology, their brother and sister academics elsewhere conduct experiments on earthquake-proof building materials and designs, weather prediction, and more. Sometimes, as in the case of earthquakes and catfish, the two lines of inquiry merge into one.

That's because prediction is neither a pure science that never fails nor a mystic craft that can succeed only by chance. The best visionaries, like the best scientists, bring knowledge and experience to their work. Scientists, like mystics, must employ imagination and creativity if they are to make predictions of lasting value. And all prophets need to bring good judgment, honesty, and open-mindedness to their work.

Finally, what of the future of prediction? One thing we can say with confidence: it will not go away. "Human life is a constant preoccupation with the future," José Ortega y Gasset wrote, and he was right. It is that preoccupation that stands between us and unknown events to come. It is that preoccupation that permits us to provide for the future and to choose the path down which the world's people are to walk.

# Bibliography

Bishop, Katherine. "Forecast for Quake Doesn't Upset a Coast Town, Which Is Used to Them." *The New York Times*, June 1, 1985.

Blakeslee, Sandra. "California at the Ready, It Hopes, for Big Quake." *The New York Times*, April 14, 1985.

———. "Volcano Warning Brings Economic Woe to Coast Resort Area." *The New York Times*, August 12, 1984.

Burmyn, Lynne, and Christina Baldwin. *Sun Signs for Kids*. New York: St. Martin's Press, 1985.

Cheetham, Erika. *The Further Prophecies of Nostradamus*. New York: The Putnam Publishing Group, 1985.

———. *The Prophecies of Nostradamus*. New York: G. P. Putnam's Sons, 1980.

Cornish, Edward, ed. *1999, The World of Tomorrow*. Washington, D.C.: World Future Society, 1978.

Cowen, Robert C. "Nuclear power plants: accident hazards have been grossly in error." *The Christian Science Monitor*, July 5, 1984.

———. "Predicting earthquakes: act wisely on long-term forecasts." *The Christian Science Monitor*, October 1, 1985.

———. "Scientists sense a breakthrough in long-range weather forecasts." *The Christian Science Monitor*, September 13, 1984.

———. "3-D computer simulations may stimulate weather forecasting." *The Christian Science Monitor*, August 27, 1985.

———. "Weathermen, not gadgets, still do the forecasting." *The Christian Science Monitor*, January 10, 1985.

Dillin, John. "Pollster: beware the political poll taken too early in race." *The Christian Science Monitor*, July 25, 1984.

Forman, Henry James. *The Story of Prophecy in the Life of Mankind from Early Times to the Present Day*. New York: Farrar & Reinhart, 1936.

Francis, David R. "The downs—or ups—of spinning out economic forecasts." *The Christian Science Monitor*, October 21, 1985.

Gallup, George, Jr., with William Proctor. *Forecast* 2000. New York: William Morrow, 1984.

Germani, Clara. "Lessons in earthquake preparedness." *The Christian Science Monitor*, April 19, 1985.

Greenwald, John. "The Forecasters Flunk." *Time*, Vol. 124, No. 9, August 27, 1984.

"Group Tries to Discern Future to Improve It." *The New York Times*, December 11, 1983.

Hall, Angus. *Signs of Things to Come*. Garden City, N.Y.: Doubleday and Company, 1975.

Hollie, Pamela G. "Coca-Cola Swallows Its Words." *The New York Times*, July 14, 1985.

———. "Fans of 'Old' Coke Wouldn't Give Up." *The New York Times*, July 12, 1985.

"Jeane Dixon: 101 Fall Predictions." *Star*, October 8, 1985.

Kerr, Richard A. "Pinning Down the Next Big California Quake." *Science*, Vol. 230, October 25, 1985.

Kramer, Samuel Noah, and the editors of Time-Life Books. *Cradle of Civilization*. New York: Time, 1967.

———. *The Sumerians: Their History, Culture and Character*. Chicago: University of Chicago Press, 1963.

Lewinsohn, Richard. *Science, Prophecy and Prediction*. New York: Harper & Row, 1961.

MacKenzie, Andrew. *Riddle of the Future: A Modern Study of Precognition*. New York: Taplinger Publishing Company, 1975.

Montgomery, Ruth. *A Gift of Prophecy: The Phenomenal Jeane Dixon*. New York: William Morrow, 1965.

"$1.25 Million Awarded in Deaths of Lobstermen." *The New York Times*, August 13, 1985.

Read, Piers Paul. *Alive*. New York: Avon Books, 1975.

Rosenbaum, David E. "Budget Forecasts? 'Pay No Attention.'" *The New York Times*, January 12, 1985.

Salisbury, David F. "A quest for quake-proof buildings." *The Christian Science Monitor*, March 17, 1984.

Sitomer, Curtis J. "Legal winds blowing afoul on government defendants." *The Christian Science Monitor*, January 10, 1985.

Spence, Lewis. *Second Sight: Its History and Origins*. London: Rider and Company, 1951.

Stevenson, Richard W. "The Revival of the 'Old' Coke." *The New York Times*, July 12, 1985.

"Study Says 4 Billion Could Starve in 'Nuclear Winter' After Attack." *The New York Times*, September 13, 1985.

Sullivan, Walter. "Big California Quake Within 50 Years Is Forecast." *The New York Times*, October 7, 1984.

———. "Sudden Blizzards: Scientists Try to Take Surprise Out of Winter." *The New York Times*, December 24, 1985.

Wilson, Colin. *They Had Strange Powers*. Garden City, N.Y.: Doubleday and Company, 1975.

# Index